Oxford School Shakespeare

Twelfth Night

edited by

Roma Gill, OBE

M.A. *Cantab*. B.Litt. *Oxon*.

Oxford University Press

Oxford University Press, Walton Street, Oxford OX2 6DP

Oxford   New York
Athens   Auckland   Bangkok   Bombay
Calcutta   Cape Town   Dar es Salaam   Delhi
Florence   Hong Kong   Istanbul   Karachi
Kuala Lumpur   Madras   Madrid   Melbourne
Mexico City   Nairobi   Paris   Singapore
Taipei   Tokyo   Toronto

and associated companies in
Berlin   Ibadan

Oxford is a trade mark of Oxford University Press

© Oxford University Press 1986
Reprinted 1988, 1990, 1991
This revised edition first published 1992
Reprinted 1993 (twice), 1994, 1995

ISBN 0 19 831974 6.

A CIP catalogue record for this book is available from the British
Library.

Illustrations by Shirley Tourret

Cover photograph by Tristram Kenton shows Donald Sumpter as
Orsino, and Harriet Walter as Viola, in the Royal Shakespeare
Company's 1988 production of *Twelfth Night*.

For Teresa

Oxford School Shakespeare
edited by Roma Gill

A Midsummer Night's Dream
Romeo and Juliet
As You Like It
Macbeth
Julius Caesar
The Merchant of Venice
Henry IV Part I
Twelfth Night
The Taming of the Shrew
Othello
Hamlet
King Lear
Henry V

Printed in Great Britain at the University Press, Cambridge

Contents

The 'Festive Season'

'Twelfth Night' is a name commonly given to the Christian Feast of the Epiphany, which is celebrated on the sixth of January (twelve days after Christmas Day) and which commemorates the coming of the Magi—the three wise men—to the stable in Bethlehem where Christ was born. They brought with them the gifts of gold, frankincense and myrrh, which were appropriate for an infant king.

Almost all societies and cultures find it necessary to have some kind of holiday in the middle of winter. The ancient Romans used to hold an annual 'Saturnalia' for about a week in the middle of December. During this period all forms of public order were suspended: the law courts and schools were closed, trading ceased, no criminals were executed, and the riotous merry-making was unrestrained. The medieval church throughout Europe adopted this festival, transferring it to the days immediately following Christmas Day (26, 27 and 28 December); on such an occasion, known as the 'Feast of Fools', the clergy in the cathedral towns would elect a boy chorister to be their 'king' for the day, whilst they feasted and made mockery of those things that they normally held sacred. In England this celebration ceased with the Reformation in the sixteenth century and its place was taken—so far as Queen Elizabeth and her court were concerned—by the 'Twelfth Night' festivities on 6 January.

The regular programme of events began in the morning when the Queen, accompanied by the entire court and her guests, attended chapel and she made a token offering of the Epiphany gifts. The religious ritual was followed by a sumptuous banquet. Then there was the entertainment.

It has been most plausibly suggested that Shakespeare's play *Twelfth Night* was first written as such an entertainment[1], and certainly anyone who has experienced Christmas television programmes will agree that all the proper amusement for a festive season is to be found in this comedy. It is, above all, *funny*. The humour is not all of the same kind: it ranges from the farce of Sir Andrew's near-duel to the slick word-play of Feste—and it allows maybe a few tears of happiness when Viola's lonely courage is rewarded by the man she loves. There is romance, in the story of Olivia as well as in the success of Viola—and even Maria has her triumph with Sir Toby. There are songs—old and new, sentimental lyrics and riotous drinking-songs. And there is dancing as the two drunken knights imitate the steps of the formal Elizabethan measures.

These elements have no date: they appeal immediately to all ages. But in other aspects *Twelfth Night* is a play of its own time, and although the topical allusions can be explained in an editor's notes, the modern readers—or audiences—cannot hope to recapture the first delight of the Elizabethans when they heard, for instance, that Malvolio, making an unaccustomed effort to smile, was creasing his face 'into more lines than is in the new map with the augmentation of the Indies' (*3*, 2, 74–6). We cannot share some of their beliefs, such as the ideas that passion was produced in the liver, and that the human body is made up of the four elements, but the twentieth century is still interested in astrology and notions that the planets might have some effect on the lives and natures of men ('Were we not born under Taurus?', *1*, 3, 128–29). The play's first audiences (whether or not Her Majesty was among them) must have been persons of exceptional wit and understanding: much of the comedy comes from allusions to an intellectual culture of remarkable complexity.

The problem of Malvolio is also solved—or ceases to be a problem—if the play is viewed in a 'festival' context. The character is cruelly treated by his enemies when they lock him in a dark room and claim that he is insane; but the treatment seems less severe if we see Malvolio as the caricature of an unpopular public figure, Sir William Knollys, the Controller of Her Majesty's Household. The official position of such a man always makes him vulnerable to satire, and it is his official duty to take it in good part.

1   In a very imaginative study by Leslie Hotson, *The First Night of 'Twelfth Night'* (London: 1954).

Leading characters in the play

Viola and Sebastian	They are twins, separated from each other in a shipwreck. Independently they arrive in Illyria where Viola, for self-protection, disguises herself as a boy and calls herself Cesario so that she can enter the service of Orsino.
Orsino	The Duke of Illyria, who can think of nothing but his love for Olivia.
Olivia	A rich countess, who rejects Orsino's love and appears to be still grieving for her brother's death.
Malvolio	The steward who is in charge of Olivia's household and aspires to marry his mistress.
Maria	Olivia's lady-in-waiting who organizes a plot against Malvolio; she is in love with Sir Toby.
Sir Toby Belch	A relation of Olivia's who has taken up residence with the countess; he disrupts the household with his drunken rioting, and proves a very expensive friend to Sir Andrew.
Sir Andrew Aguecheek	A foolish knight whose name suggests his appearance (shivers and pallor are symptoms of the *ague* = a malarial fever).
Feste	A professional jester who serves Olivia as an official fool, but also moves freely between her house and the Duke's palace. He interprets the characters and seems to comment on the action rather than participating in it.
Scene	Illyria: the action moves between Orsino's court and Olivia's house.

Twelfth Night: commentary

Act 1

Scene 1 In his rich ducal palace the young Orsino seems bored and depressed; he calls for music, but is immediately tired of the tune. Other members of his company try to amuse him—this is, after all, their job. They are not really Orsino's friends but courtiers, attendant lords like Curio who must address their master with respect as 'my lord', smile at his wit in the word-play on 'hart' and 'heart', and show admiration for the clever way in which he compares himself to Actaeon (the hunter in Greek mythology who was turned into a stag and pursued by his own hounds). Orsino fancies that he is in love with Olivia, and his passion increases when he hears, once again, that she has refused to entertain his messenger.

  The atmosphere of the short scene seems overheated. Orsino talks most, and his tones are languid and meditative. He leaves the stage in search of 'sweet beds of flowers' where he can lie and indulge his day-dreams.

Scene 2 The next scene brings a breath of fresh salt sea air as the characters—Viola and those who have escaped with her from a shipwreck—speak with urgency: they have just escaped death by drowning, and must now make plans for their survival. Viola's first thought is for her brother; he is still missing but Viola refuses to believe that he is dead. The Captain tries to encourage her hope, and helps her to plot her immediate future in this foreign country. She makes a vigorous start towards a new life: 'Lead me on'.

Scene 3 The first two scenes contrasted, through the movement of the verse, the ineffectual languor of Orsino's court and the realistic energy with which Viola reacts to the loneliness of her new situation. A change to prose in the third scene heralds comedy, as Sir Toby Belch discusses with Maria the accomplishments of his friend, Sir Andrew Aguecheek, who is being presented as a suitor for Olivia. Maria has a sharp answer to every one of Sir Toby's remarks in praise of his friend, and when Sir Andrew appears on the scene we are prepared to find 'a very fool and a prodigal'. Sir Andrew does not disappoint our expectations, making a clumsy attempt—prompted by Sir Toby—to flirt with Maria. He is himself, however, dissatisfied with Olivia's rejection of him, and threatens to leave Illyria—to Sir Toby's dismay. Sir Toby, we realize, has been glad to have Sir Andrew's presence, because he has been drinking at the thin knight's expense and cannot afford to lose him now! With gross flattery, he persuades Sir Andrew that Olivia must love him for his accomplishments; and the scene ends as the two knights caper around the stage in a parody of all the most elegant Elizabethan dances.

These first three scenes have introduced us to the three main situations in the play: to the love-sick depression of Orsino in his ducal palace; to the loneliness of Viola, cast ashore on a foreign coast; and to the jollity of Olivia's house (although this is not shared by its owner, who is still unknown). After these introductions, the action of the play is ready to begin.

Scene 4   Disguised as a boy, and calling herself Cesario, Viola has won the trust and respect of her master, who has confided in her all the secrets of his love for Olivia. Now Viola is to be his go-between and messenger to the two parties. But there is a major complication, for Viola finds that there is a terrible conflict between her duty to her master and her own desires: she is sent to court Olivia on Orsino's behalf—'a barful strife! Whoe'er I woo, myself would be his wife'.

Scene 5   Again, the change to prose signals a more relaxed attitude, although the wit is now intellectual, demanding quicker responses from the audience than the early comic capers of Sir Toby and Sir Andrew. Maria is trying to force a confession from Feste, but she is no match for the professional jester. Feste next proceeds to demonstrate his skill before Olivia, using the syllogistic arguments beloved of Elizabethan scholars. With a daring parody of the catechism of the Church of England, he proves that it is his mistress, and not himself, who is the real fool. His wit, however, does not amuse Malvolio, who as Olivia's steward is responsible for the proper conduct of her household. It is a position of importance, and one which inevitably creates enemies amongst those who must be disciplined. But even Olivia finds that the steward is somewhat too strict, over-reacting to any supposed affront to his dignity: 'O you are sick of self-love, Malvolio, and taste with a distempered appetite'. When Malvolio has left the stage, however, she warns Feste that some people dislike his fooling—but he seems to place himself under her protection, and helps her to handle the drunken Sir Toby.

Malvolio returns to the stage to describe, with disdain, the persistence of the latest ambassador from Orsino. Intrigued by such determination, Olivia agrees to allow him access—but tries to deceive him by appearing, like Maria, in a veil.

Viola/Cesario starts her wooing with a most elegant speech—but after only the first line her common sense asserts itself and she insists upon knowing the identity of her listeners, being reluctant to 'cast away' on a waiting-woman the speech that she has so carefully composed and taken so much trouble to learn by heart. Having resisted Maria's attempt to force her departure, it is Viola who succeeds in dismissing both Maria and all the attendants, so that she is left alone with Olivia. The veil is drawn, and Viola looks on Olivia's beauty. Her comments do not seem forced and exaggerated (as we would expect from Orsino's praise); Viola looks for traces of cosmetics—which the Elizabethans deplored—and when she can find no evidence of such painting, she speaks to Olivia with candour:

> 'Tis beauty truly blent, whose red and white
> Nature's own sweet and cunning hand laid on.

Olivia is surprised, but retaliates with a spirited fancifulness and pretends that her beauty is to be sold at an auction. When Viola describes how *she* would demonstrate her love, it is clear that Olivia is much attracted to Orsino's messenger, and Viola's scorn when she is offered payment makes her still more attractive. The device of the ring declares Olivia's passion even more plainly than her confused words at the end of the scene.

Act 2

Scene 1   Just as the plot begins to get tangled, Shakespeare gives us an indication that all will end happily; somehow, Sebastian will save the situation. He is not dead, but alive and in Illyria. This very careful prose scene makes us sure of his identity—and throughout the rest of the play we can laugh with confidence at the problems of the other characters because we know that there will be a happy resolution for them.

Sebastian has found a true friend in Antonio, the sea-captain who rescued him from the shipwreck. Although he is a very minor figure in the play, Antonio is a much-valued character for the unselfish generosity and humility with which he follows the fortunes of his young master.

Scene 2   Quite unlike the sea-captain is Malvolio, Olivia's steward, who now shows his self-esteem and arrogance in the contempt with which he tries to give his mistress's ring to Viola. After he has flounced off the stage, Viola meditates on the meaning of the ring; she interprets correctly, and neatly summarizes the confusions caused by love and her own disguise:

> As I am man,
> My state is desperate for my master's love:
> As I am woman (now, alas the day!)
> What thriftless sighs shall poor Olivia breathe?

Any momentary pathos evoked by this predicament is immediately forgotten in the noisy laughter of the next scene.

Scene 3   Sir Toby and Sir Andrew have been drinking, and although it is well after midnight they persuade Feste to sing for them and then all join in a noisy chorus, ignoring Maria's warnings. They even scoff at Malvolio, who has been sent by Olivia to silence their riotous behaviour and who, when they will not obey, returns to his mistress to report on their contempt. The guilty merrymakers (perhaps a little afraid and subdued at Malvolio's words) plan to make a fool of the steward in revenge for his scolding. And Sir Toby asks Sir Andrew for still more money. The knights go off for another drink, having decided that it is 'too late to go to bed now'.

Scene 4   The action sobers again in this scene as Orsino bids 'good morrow, friends' and calls for *his* kind of music; Feste again will be the singer when the raucous drinking-songs change to tender love-lyrics. But before he arrives from Olivia's house, Orsino and Viola begin their debate on the nature of love which is the central subject of this scene. Orsino speaks for all romantic lovers: Viola is a realist. She takes this opportunity, however, of declaring her love for the duke; the audience understands the real meaning of her words, although Orsino (who believes himself to be addressing his page, Cesario) is deceived by the references to the page's 'sister' whose history is 'A blank' and who 'never told her love'. In this scene the actress who plays the part of Viola sometimes presents the character as though she were asking for our sympathy—pity for the plight of a lonely orphan, with no protective brother or friends, hopelessly in love with a man to whom she cannot reveal her secret passion. But this is not Viola as I understand the character. I see a resolute young woman who faces the difficulties of her situation with energy and wit, refusing to be a victim of circumstances and even determined—from the very beginning of the play—that Orsino is the man who can help her: on first hearing his name (in Scene 2) her reaction suggests a plan:

> Orsino! I have heard my father name him:
> He was a bachelor then.

Viola is not a *simple* character; like all Shakespeare's best creations, she is a mixture of different, even contradictory, qualities—just like most real human beings!

As soon as it has aroused Orsino's interest, the pathetic little story of Cesario's 'sister' ends—with a riddle which is plain enough to the spectators of the play but puzzling to Orsino; and even Viola/Cesario does not know the full meaning of her words:

> I am all the daughters of my father's house,
> And all the brothers too; and yet I know not. . .

When Viola speaks of love she does not use the extravagant language that characterizes Orsino's passion: her words are simple, direct and sincere. We could almost forget—for the moment—that we are watching a play.

Scene 5   Now the action changes into a comedy which is highly *theatrical*, where we are expected to believe that this is Olivia's garden and that the two knights (with their friend Fabian) are hidden in the thick bush of the box-tree. Yet though they are concealed from

Malvolio's view, their words and actions are evident to the audience, who must remember that Sir Andrew himself has aspirations to Olivia's hand, whilst they cannot forget that Malvolio (despite his proud self-righteousness) is merely Olivia's steward and not her social equal.

The comedy starts with Malvolio's day-dreaming—and the comments of the onlookers. It is not love for Olivia that motivates his actions, but the ambition 'To be Count Malvolio' and show disdain for 'my kinsman Toby'. These characteristics are demonstrated *before* Malvolio finds the forged letter—preparing the audience for his attempts to decipher its message to suit his own wishes. Maria's device succeeds; and when she returns at the end of the scene it is to lead us all—the audience as well as the spectators behind the box-hedge—on to the next episode when Malvolio will appear before Olivia

in yellow stockings, and 'tis a colour she abhors; and cross-gartered, a fashion she detests; and he will smile upon her, which will now be so unsuitable to her disposition...

Act 3

Scene 1   Now Shakespeare begins to interweave his different plots, introducing Viola/Cesario to the two knights. She is already familiar with Feste, whom she encountered briefly at Orsino's court. Here she speaks directly to the jester, showing a wit that is almost a match for his professional talents. This is a new aspect of Viola's character: the shipwrecked 'damsel in distress' could not have joked in this light-hearted manner, and it would have been inappropriate—even impertinent—for 'Cesario' to talk like this in Orsino's presence. Feste cleverly begs for money, which is readily given because it has been *earned* by the fool's talent. Viola's words, when she is alone, show her respect for the professional skill of the clown and for the 'folly which he wisely shows'—which is quite different from the stupidity of some apparently 'wise men'—i.e. men who claim to be sensible and who would scorn a fool.

Such a man now appears, when Sir Andrew attempts to create a good impression with his French greeting. He seems to be disconcerted by Viola's quick retort (probably spoken with a better French accent than his own), and his admiration increases when the Duke's page addresses Olivia in words that Sir Andrew could never have found for himself. It is only a brief encounter—just long enough for Sir Andrew to realize that he now has a rival.

The more serious business of the scene follows when Olivia is left alone with the person whom she knows as 'Cesario' and to whom she now declares her love. The situation is embarrassing for both characters—for Olivia because she must speak of love to a 'man' who is socially inferior to her, and for Viola because she must hear these sentiments and react to them as though she were indeed a man. She manages to handle the interview with an elegant dignity, always remaining loyal to her master, Orsino, and speaking frankly to Olivia ('you do think you are not what you are'). She hints at a mystery ('I am not what I am'), and departs with grace and sincerity in her voice ('By innocence I swear, and by my youth').

Scene 2   It appears, however, that there has been a witness of this scene who, although he could not hear what was spoken, has taken great offence at what he has seen: 'I saw your niece do more favours to the Count's servingman than ever she bestowed upon me'. Sir Toby flatters Sir Andrew with a new interpretation of the episode, provoking him to fight the duke's page (or, at least, to challenge Cesario to a duel). The scene is written in a fast-moving prose, packed so densely with jests that a contemporary audience would not have had time to breathe between the laughs. Then Maria calls us all to 'laugh (y)ourselves into stitches' at the sight of Malvolio, fooled by the letter into the costume and conduct that were recommended to him.

Scene 3   But just before the comedy proceeds, Shakespeare inserts another scene with Sebastian that reassures us, helping the audience to anticipate the play's happy ending. The verse is simple and straightforward as Antonio explains why he cannot accompany Sebastian on his sight-seeing tour of the city. The short scene provides a little interval—a rest in the laughter—before the comedy reaches its height with the complications of misunderstanding and mistaken identity.

Scene 4 Olivia speaks first, in words that are not intended to be overheard, wondering how to receive Cesario. She sends for Malvolio and hears from Maria that the steward is acting very strangely and may even be 'possessed' by the devil—in other words, completely and dangerously mad. Malvolio's appearance confirms this report: he is strangely dressed and speaks to his mistress with leering hints quite foreign to his usual formal manners. When he is briefly alone, Malvolio's soliloquy shows the extent to which he flatters himself. Sir Toby approaches, picking up Maria's suggestion that Malvolio is insane and speaking as if to a child. After Malvolio leaves the stage, the three conspirators (Fabian has accompanied Sir Toby) comment on the success of their device with the observation that

> If this were played upon a stage now, I could condemn it as an improbable fiction.

This remark perhaps prevents the theatre audience from voicing the same idea!

The treatment—or punishment—that is now planned for Malvolio is the usual Elizabethan prescription for madness; Malvolio is to be kept in darkness and bound until the devil leaves him. Another form of insanity—'More matter for a May morning'—is introduced when Sir Andrew brings the letter of challenge. Shakespeare now returns to Viola, marking the transition with a change from prose to verse which allows for a momentary seriousness as Olivia declares her love. Another comic misunderstanding follows (with a return to prose) when Sir Toby delivers his friend's challenge to Viola; and the comedy is redoubled when he returns to Sir Andrew. But the duel is stopped before it has started by the sudden and unexpected intervention of Antonio. This is a brilliant theatrical stroke, all the more effective because, on looking back at the play, we can see that Shakespeare has in fact prepared us for this moment, first by introducing Antonio as the friend of Sebastian (Viola's identical twin), and then by showing us how and why the two friends have separated from each other.

But the next episode is a sorrowful one for Antonio, when he is arrested at Sir Toby's command—and we must remember that he told Sebastian that Illyria is a dangerous town for him: 'if I be lapsed in this place, I shall pay dear' (*3*, 3, 36–7). Even though we understand the mistake, we must feel great sympathy with him when Viola cannot return his purse: Antonio is risking his life to help the boy—Sebastian—whom he loves; and it now appears that he is rejected and refused in his moment of need:

> But Oh how vile an idol proves this god!
> Thou hast, Sebastian, done good feature shame.

His mention of her brother's name raises Viola's hopes at once, and we can see that her problems will soon be solved. But there are still more mistakes to come—and also more comedy.

Act 4

Scene 1   Sebastian is now drawn into one of the play's major plots; he encounters Feste—and is of course mistaken for Viola/Cesario, who is completely identical in dress and appearance. But the twins *are* clearly distinguished from each other by their manner of speech: when Viola jested with Feste in *Act 3*, Scene 1 she spoke to the fool with a witty sophistication that almost equalled his own, whereas Sebastian, in the present scene, shows impatience with Feste's fooling. The same impatience characterizes his reactions to Sir Andrew and Sir Toby—who also mistake him for 'Cesario'. Finally Olivia receives Sebastian as though he were the one she loves, speaking her sincerity in verse. And Sebastian, enchanted, responds to her: 'If it be thus to dream, still let me sleep'.

Scene 2   The next scene is not a dream but a nightmare! Most comedy involves pain of some kind: the spectators laugh, but the person who is the object of the laughter may not share the enjoyment. Here Maria and Sir Toby take pleasure in duping Malvolio, and Feste has a double delight, both exercising his acting skill *and* taking revenge on Malvolio. But we begin to feel sorry for the steward, tormented so expertly by his enemies and powerless to help himself. The clowning is brilliant—but it begins to hurt. Already Sir Toby is beginning to feel uneasy: 'I would we were well rid of this knavery'. When Feste sheds his disguise and taunts Malvolio in his own voice, the steward pleads with the fool, but there is still some dignity in his request—and it seems as though Feste will not stop the torture until all Malvolio's pride is gone and he begs for Feste's help, promising to 'requite it in the highest degree'.

Scene 3　As Feste sings himself off the stage, a bewildered Sebastian appears, musing at his sudden good fortune. There is nevertheless a sense of urgency in the verse, especially when he is joined by Olivia who intends instant marriage.

Act 5

Scene 1　After a light-hearted battle of wits between Orsino and Feste (in which Feste cleverly begs two coins from the Duke) the comedy seems to be threatened with seriousness. Antonio was speaking the truth when, separating from Sebastian in *Act 3*, Scene 2, he told the boy that he would 'pay dear' if he should be arrested in Illyria. Orsino is stern—although even in his censure of Antonio he acknowledges the 'fame and honour' of the captain.

But confusions, complications and explanations follow fast upon each other: Viola is claimed as Sebastian, his friend, by Antonio and as Cesario, her newly-wed husband, by Olivia; she is threatened as a rival by both Orsino and Sir Andrew; and she is finally recognized as herself by her brother. The changing moods of the scene are most strongly marked by the changes from verse to prose; and the pace varies from the speed with which Sir Toby and Sir Andrew are dismissed to the slow caution of the verse that reveals the identities of the shipwrecked twins. Olivia claims her husband, and Orsino looks to find a wife in his former page, reminding Viola that, as Cesario, she had said 'a thousand times Thou never shouldst love woman like to me'. Verse again gives way to prose when Malvolio is remembered and the facts about his 'madness' are revealed by Feste and Fabian, but the comedy ends with a dignified verse speech from the ill-used steward. The speech declares his presumptuous ambitions as well as his injuries, and is itself enough to answer his question: 'Tell me why?'. But Malvolio has not learned the lesson that the deception was intended to teach him, and he leaves the stage in a bad temper, determined on revenge. He alone is excluded from the general happiness which unites the other characters.

The play ends with a song from Feste which insists on 'the wind and the rain' of everyday life, directing the audience away from the crazy, enchanted realm of Illyria because now 'our play is done'. It is time for applause.

The Sources of *Twelfth Night*

The immediate source for Shakespeare's play is a prose narrative, 'The Tale of Apolonius and Silla', which was told by Barnabe Riche in *Riche his Farewell to Militarie Profession* (1581). Riche tells how Silla loved Duke Apolonius, 'a very young man' whom she had met at her father's house in Cyprus. He was a soldier, however, and took no notice of the girl's attentions. Eventually he returned to his home in Constantinople. Silla followed him, but her ship was wrecked in a storm. She managed to save herself by clinging to a sea-chest, and on reaching land she disguised herself as a boy (in clothes that she found in the same chest) and went to Duke Apolonius. She offered to serve him as a page, calling herself by the name of her own brother, 'Silvio'.

'"Silvio" pleased his master so well, that above all the rest of his servants about him, he had the greatest credit, and the Duke put him most in trust' (see *1*, 4, 1–15).

Apolonius sent his page with love-messages to a widow, Julina, but she rejected the Duke's appeals — and instead fell in love with 'Silvio'. One day, however, the *real* Silvio came to Constantinople in search of his sister, Silla. Julina (mistaking him for the Duke's page) invited him into her house. They made love, and Julina became pregnant; but the next day Silvio left the city. Apolonius proposed marriage to Julina, but she told him of another man, 'whose wife I now remain by faithful vow and promise'. When her pregnancy became apparent, Julina named 'Silvio' as the father of her child. Apolonius threatened to kill his page, but Silla revealed herself to Julina, telling how she had left her father's house and sailed across the sea because of her love for Apolonius. On hearing this, the Duke married Silla — and as soon as her brother learned what had happened, he came back to Constantinople and wedded Julina.

This story did not originate with Barnabe Riche. He found it, in a slightly different form, in a collection of tales[1] by a French writer, Belleforest; and Belleforest made his version from the story told by an Italian writer, Bandello[2]. The ultimate source for these narratives is an anonymous Italian play, *Gl'Ingannati* (*The Deceived Ones*), which was performed in 1531 and published at Venice in 1537.

[1] *Histoires Tragiques*, Part IV, No. 59 (1570).
[2] *Novelle*, Part II, No. 36 (1554).

Shakespeare's Verse

Shakespeare's plays are mainly written in 'blank verse', the form preferred by most dramatists in the sixteenth and early seventeenth centuries. It is a very flexible medium, which is capable — like the human speaking voice — of a wide range of tones. Basically the lines, which are unrhymed, are ten syllables long. The syllables have alternating stresses, just like normal English speech; and they divide into five 'feet'. The technical name for this is 'iambic pentameter'.

Orsino
If músic bé the foód of love, play on,
Give mé excess of it, that, surfeiting,
The áppetíte may sicken, and so dié.
That stráin agaín, it hád a dýing fáll;
O, it came o'ér my eaŕ like thé sweet soúnd
That bréathes upon a bank of violéts,
Stéaling and gíving ódour. Enough, no moŕe;
'Tis nót so sweét now aś it waś befoŕe.
O spírit of love, how quick and frésh art thóu,
That nótwithstanding thý capácitý
Recéiveth aś the séa, nought enters thére,
Of whát validitý and pítch soe'ér,
But fálls intó abátement and low príce
Even in á minúte! So fúll of shapes is fancy,
That ít alone is high fantásticál.
Curio
Will yoú go hunt, my lord?
Orsino
                                    What, Cúrio?
Curio
The haŕt.
Orsino
Why só I dó, the nóblest thát I have.

I, i, i–18

Here the pentameter accommodates a variety of speech tones — the careful regularity of the first lines emphasizes Orsino's self-conscious pose as the romantic lover, delivering beautifully prepared thoughts. His lyrical ecstasy swoons over the 'bank of violets'; it is dismissed with the abrupt 'Enough, no more'; and then it develops into a highly philosophical meditation about the nature of love. Curio's suggestion, 'Will you go hunt, my lord?', brings in a note of commonsense — perhaps even of exasperation! Orsino is quick to respond, sharing in the same pentameter as Curio.

In this quotation, the lines are mainly regular in length and normal in iambic stress pattern. Sometimes Shakespeare deviates from the norm, writing lines that are longer or shorter than ten syllables, and varying the stress patterns for unusual emphasis ('Stéaling and gíving oďour. Enoúgh, no moŕe'). The verse line sometimes contains the grammatical unit of meaning — ''Tis nót so swéet now aś it wás befoŕe' — thus allowing for a pause at the end of the line, before a new idea is started; at other times, the sense runs on from one line to the next — 'tȟy capácitý Recéiveth aś the séa'. This makes for the natural fluidity of speech, avoiding monotony but still maintaining the iambic rhythm.

Date and Text

Twelfth Night must have been written at some time between 1599 and 1602. Evidence for the first date, the *terminus a quo*, comes from a topical allusion in *Act 3*, Scene 2, where Malvolio's smiling face is said to be creased into 'more lines than is in the new map with the augmentation of the Indies' (lines 75–6). This map was published in 1599. The second date, the *terminus ad quem*, is supplied by a law-student, John Manningham, who recorded in his Diary a production that he had witnessed at a feast in the Middle Temple, but it is unlikely that this was the play's first performance. The name of Shakespeare's love-sick Duke might provide an additional clue for dating the play: in the winter of 1600–1601 a noble visitor was entertained at the court of Queen Elizabeth — Don Virginio Orsino, Duke of Bracciano.

Twelfth Night was not published until 1623, when it appeared in the First Folio collection of Shakespeare's plays.

Characters in the Play

Viola (*later disguised as* Cesario) ⎫
Sebastian (Viola's *brother*) ⎭ *twins shipwrecked on the coast of* Illyria

Captain   *the ship's captain, who rescued* Viola
Antonio   *another captain, who befriended* Sebastian

Orsino   Duke of Illyria
Valentine ⎫
Curio ⎭ *Gentlemen attending on the* Duke

Olivia   *a countess, living in* Illyria
Maria   Olivia's *lady-in-waiting*
Feste   Olivia's *fool*
Malvolio   *steward of* Olivia's *household*
Fabian   *a member of* Olivia's *household*

Sir Toby Belch   Olivia's *uncle*
Sir Andrew Aguecheek   Sir Toby's *friend*

A Servant
A Priest

Sailors, Attendants, Musicians, Officers

Location

The action of the play takes place in Illyria, a country (now Yugoslavia) on the eastern side of the Adriatic. Viola and Sebastian are shipwrecked (separately) on its coast, and make their way to an unnamed city where Olivia lives and where the Duke has his palace.

Act I

Scene I *The Duke's court*

[Music] Enter Orsino, *Duke of Illyria,*
Curio, *and Attendants*

Orsino
If music be the food of love, play on,
Give me excess of it, that, surfeiting,
The appetite may sicken, and so die.
That strain again, it had a dying fall:
5 O, it came o'er my ear like the sweet sound
That breathes upon a bank of violets,
Stealing and giving odour. Enough, no more;
'Tis not so sweet now as it was before.
O spirit of love, how quick and fresh art thou,
10 That notwithstanding thy capacity
Receiveth as the sea, nought enters there,
Of what validity and pitch soe'er,
But falls into abatement and low price
Even in a minute! So full of shapes is fancy,
15 That it alone is high fantastical.
    Curio
Will you go hunt, my lord?
    Orsino   What, Curio?
    Curio
The hart.
    Orsino
Why so I do, the noblest that I have.
O, when mine eyes did see Olivia first,
20 Methought she purg'd the air of pestilence;
That instant was I turn'd into a hart,
And my desires, like fell and cruel hounds,
E'er since pursue me.

    Enter Valentine
              How now? What news from her?

24   'I'm sorry to have to tell you, my lord, but I was not admitted into the house.'

26   *The element itself*: even the air (or sky).

till seven years' heat: until seven summers are past.

27   *at ample view*: in full sight (i.e. without a veil).

28   *cloistress*: nun (in an enclosed order).

30   *eye-offending brine*: salt tears that sting the eyes.

season: keep fresh (as brine is used to preserve meat and vegetables).

32   *remembrance*: Shakespeare in fact uses an old form of this word, 'rememberance'—which provides the additional syllable for his metrical line.

33   *that fine frame*: so sensitively formed.

34   *but*: merely.

35   *shaft*: arrow; Cupid (the god of love) had two kinds of arrow: the one with the golden tip caused love, whilst the leaden arrow brought hatred.

36   *all affections else*: all other emotions.

37-9   'When there is only one ruler (*one self king*) who occupies the royal (*sovereign*) thrones in those *sweet perfections*—her liver, brain, and heart (which the Elizabethans believed to be the seats of passion, thoughts and emotions).'

Valentine
So please my lord, I might not be admitted,
25 But from her handmaid do return this answer:
The element itself, till seven years' heat,
Shall not behold her face at ample view;
But like a cloistress she will veiled walk,
And water once a day her chamber round
30 With eye-offending brine: all this to season
A brother's dead love, which she would keep fresh
And lasting, in her sad remembrance.
    Orsino
O, she that hath a heart of that fine frame
To pay this debt of love but to a brother,
35 How will she love, when the rich golden shaft
Hath kill'd the flock of all affections else
That live in her; when liver, brain, and heart,
These sovereign thrones, are all supplied, and fill'd
Her sweet perfections with one self king!
40 Away before me to sweet beds of flowers!
Love-thoughts lie rich when canopied with
    bowers.

[*Exeunt*

Act I   Scene 2
A ship has been wrecked off the coast of Illyria. Viola and her twin brother Sebastian were passengers on the ship, and although Viola, with some of the sailors, has survived, there is no news of Sebastian. Alone, and a stranger in Illyria, Viola decides to dress as a boy and offer her services to Orsino.

4   *Elysium*: in Greek mythology, this was the home of the blessed in the after-life. Viola fears that her brother is now dead.

Scene 2 *The sea-coast*

Enter Viola, *a* Captain, *and* Sailors
    Viola
What country, friends, is this?
    Captain
This is Illyria, lady.
    Viola
And what should I do in Illyria?
My brother he is in Elysium.
5 Perchance he is not drown'd: what think you, sailors?

It is perchance that you yourself were sav'd.
    Viola
O my poor brother! and so perchance may he be.
    Captain
True, madam, and to comfort you with chance,
Assure yourself, after our ship did split,
10 When you and those poor number sav'd with you
Hung on our driving boat, I saw your brother,
Most provident in peril, bind himself
(Courage and hope both teaching him the practice)
To a strong mast that liv'd upon the sea;
15 Where, like Arion on the dolphin's back,
I saw him hold acquaintance with the waves
So long as I could see.
    Viola
For saying so, there's gold:
Mine own escape unfoldeth to my hope,
20 Whereto thy speech serves for authority,
The like of him. Know'st thou this country?

5   *Perchance*: perhaps; *and also* 'by good fortune'—as in line 6.

8   *chance*: possibility.
9   *Assure yourself*: be assured.
10   *poor number*: few.
11   *driving*: drifting.

13   *the practice*: what to do.
14   *liv'd*: floated.

15   *Arion*: a Greek musician who was carried to safety by a dolphin after he had thrown himself into the sea to escape murderous sailors.
16   *hold acquaintance*: maintain friendly contact (i.e. without sinking).
19   *unfoldeth to*: encourages me in.
21   *The like of him*: that the same has happened to him.

Captain

Ay, madam, well, for I was bred and born
Not three hours' travel from this very place.

Viola

Who governs here?

Captain

25 A noble duke, in nature as in name.

Viola

What is his name?

Captain

Orsino.

Viola

Orsino! I have heard my father name him.
He was a bachelor then.

Captain

30 And so is now, or was so very late;
For but a month ago I went from hence,
And then 'twas fresh in murmur (as, you know,
What great ones do, the less will prattle of)
That he did seek the love of fair Olivia.

Viola

35 What's she?

Captain ·

A virtuous maid, the daughter of a count
That died some twelvemonth since; then leaving
    her
In the protection of his son, her brother,
Who shortly also died; for whose dear love
40 (They say) she hath abjur'd the company
And sight of men.

Viola   O that I serv'd that lady,
And might not be deliver'd to the world,
Till I had made mine own occasion mellow,
What my estate is.

Captain   That were hard to compass,
45 Because she will admit no kind of suit,
No, not the Duke's.

Viola

There is a fair behaviour in thee, Captain;
And though that nature with a beauteous wall
Doth oft close in pollution, yet of thee
50 I will believe thou hast a mind that suits
With this thy fair and outward character.

30   *very late*: quite recently.

32   *fresh in murmur*: newly rumoured.

33   *prattle of*: gossip about.

40   *abjur'd*: renounced.

42   *deliver'd to the world*: made known to the world.

43   'Until I considered that the time was ripe.'

44   *estate*: position (social and financial).
    compass: arrange.

45   *admit*: take notice of.
    suit: request.

47   *fair behaviour*: honest appearance.

48   *though that*: although.

50   *will*: am prepared to.

51   *character*: appearance.

53   *Conceal*: disguise.
      what I am: my real nature (i.e.
as a woman).

54   *haply shall become*: may chance
to suit.

57   *worth thy pains*: i.e. the Captain
himself might benefit.

58   *many sorts*: i.e. instrumental as
well as vocal.

59   *allow*: prove.
      worth: suitable for.

60   *hap*: happen.

61   *shape*: adapt.

62   *mute*: dumb servants (such as
were regularly employed—along with
eunuchs—in eastern countries).

63   *blabs*: tells tales.
      let . . . see: put out my eyes.

I prithee (and I'll pay thee bounteously)
Conceal me what I am, and be my aid
For such disguise as haply shall become
55 The form of my intent. I'll serve this duke;
Thou shalt present me as an eunuch to him—
It may be worth thy pains—for I can sing,
And speak to him in many sorts of music,
That will allow me very worth his service.
60 What else may hap, to time I will commit;
Only shape thou thy silence to my wit.
      Captain
Be you his eunuch, and your mute I'll be:
When my tongue blabs, then let mine eyes not see.
      Viola
I thank thee. Lead me on.   [*Exeunt*

Act 1   Scene 3
Sir Toby Belch, Olivia's kinsman, has
taken up residence in her house with
his friend, Sir Andrew Aguecheek.
Their riotous conduct is disturbing the
entire household and Maria advises Sir
Toby to mend his ways. The two are
discussing Sir Andrew and his follies
when Aguecheek arrives; he tries to
flirt with Maria, and he is flattered by
Sir Toby's praise—not realizing that he
is being ridiculed. Sir Andrew's real
ambition is to marry Olivia.

1   *What a plague*: what the devil.
      niece and *cousin* in line 4, are
used vaguely and indicate no precise
relationship between Olivia and Sir
Toby.

3   *troth*: faith.

4   *takes great exceptions*: objects
very strongly.

5   *ill hours*: irregular habits.

6   *let her except*: let her make
objections.
      except, before excepted: Sir Toby
uses a legal expression merely for fun:
there is no particular meaning. (The
Latin phrase is *exceptis excipiendis*—

Scene 3 Olivia's *house*

Enter Sir Toby Belch *and* Maria

      Sir Toby
What a plague means my niece to take the death of
her brother thus? I am sure care's an enemy to life.
      Maria
By my troth, Sir Toby, you must come in earlier o'
nights: your cousin, my lady, takes great exceptions
5 to your ill hours.
      Sir Toby
Why, let her except, before excepted.
      Maria
Ay, but you must confine yourself within the
modest limits of order.
      Sir Toby
Confine? I'll confine myself no finer than I am.
10 These clothes are good enough to drink in, and so
be these boots too—an' they be not, let them hang
themselves in their own straps.
      Maria
That quaffing and drinking will undo you. I heard
my lady talk of it yesterday, and of a foolish knight
15 that you brought in one night here to be her wooer.

'excepting those things which are to be excepted'.)

7   *confine*: restrict.
         modest limits of order: bounds of decent behaviour.

9   Sir Toby pretends that 'confine' refers to his way of dressing—and refuses to dress in any more fine clothing than he already wears.

11   *an if*.

11–12   *let them ... straps*: this is Sir Toby's variation of the common Elizabethan expression of contemptuous dismissal: 'hang yourself in your own garters'.

13   *quaffing*: heavy drinking.
         undo: ruin

18   *tall*: brave; but in line 19 Maria pretends that Sir Andrew's height is being described.
         as any's in Illyria: as any man in Illyria.

20   *ducats*: gold coins.

21   *have but a year ... ducats*: only keep all these ducats for a year.

23   *viol-de-gamboys*: bass-viol.

25   *without book*: i.e. he knows the languages by heart.

Sir Toby
Who, Sir Andrew Aguecheek?
Maria
Aye, he.
Sir Toby
He's as tall a man as any's in Illyria.
Maria
What's that to th' purpose?
Sir Toby
20   Why, he has three thousand ducats a year.
Maria
Ay, but he'll have but a year in all these ducats, he's a very fool, and a prodigal.
Sir Toby
Fie that you'll say so! He plays o' th' viol-de-gamboys, and speaks three or four languages word
25   for word without book, and hath all the good gifts of nature.

27   *natural*: as an idiot, a born fool or 'natural'.

29   *gift of a coward*: talent for cowardice.
         allay: modify.
         gust: enjoyment.

31   *gift of a grave*: be given a grave (i.e. be killed).

Maria
He hath indeed all, most natural: for besides that he's a fool, he's a great quarreller; and but that he hath the gift of a coward to allay the gust he hath in
30   quarrelling, 'tis thought among the prudent he would quickly have the gift of a grave.

32 *substractors*: Sir Toby has invented the word, giving it the meaning of 'detractors' (= those who diminish a reputation); 'substract', however, is a form of 'subtract'—so Maria can play on this in the next line.

38 *coistrel*: villain.
39 *turn o' th' toe*: spin round.
40 *parish top*: a large top was kept in the villages to make exercise and entertainment for the peasants.
  Castiliano vulgo: this phrase has never been satisfactorily explained; the context suggests that Maria is being told to look serious and not let Sir Andrew—who is approaching—guess that they have been talking about him.
41 *Agueface*: Sir Toby scoffs at both the name and appearance of Sir Andrew (see p. vi).
44 *shrew*: a mouse-like animal; probably Sir Andrew intends the word as a term of affection for the diminutive Maria—but it was usually applied to a scolding, ill-tempered woman.
46 *Accost*: speak courteously; but Sir Andrew thinks (line 49) that this is Maria's name.

53 *front*: confront, approach directly.
  board her: get on good terms with her.
55 *undertake*: tackle; Sir Andrew appreciates the sexual innuendoes in Sir Toby's verbs.
  in this company: in front of all these people.

Sir Toby
By this hand, they are scoundrels and substractors that say so of him. Who are they?
Maria
They that add, moreover, he's drunk nightly in 35 your company.
Sir Toby
With drinking healths to my niece: I'll drink to her as long as there is a passage in my throat, and drink in Illyria. He's a coward and a coistrel that will not drink to my niece till his brains turn o' th' toe, 40 like a parish top. What, wench! *Castiliano vulgo*: for here comes Sir Andrew Agueface.

Enter Sir Andrew Aguecheek

Sir Andrew
Sir Toby Belch! How now, Sir Toby Belch?
Sir Toby
Sweet Sir Andrew!
Sir Andrew
Bless you, fair shrew.
Maria
45 And you too, sir.
Sir Toby
Accost, Sir Andrew, accost.
Sir Andrew
What's that?
Sir Toby
My niece's chambermaid.
Sir Andrew
Good Mistress Accost, I desire better 50 acquaintance.
Maria
My name is Mary, sir.
Sir Andrew
Good Mistress Mary Accost—
Sir Toby
You mistake, knight. 'Accost' is front her, board her, woo her, assail her.
Sir Andrew
55 By my troth, I would not undertake her in this company. Is that the meaning of 'accost'?

58   *An*: if.
62   *in hand*: to deal with.
63–74   This banter between Maria and
Sir Andrew is a sexual flirtation which
a mere verbal paraphrase is inadequate
to convey.
63   *I have ... hand*: I am not
holding your hand.
64   *Marry*: a mild oath (= by [the
Virgin] Mary).
65   *thought is free*: the usual retort
to the question 'Do you take me for a
fool?'.
66   *buttery bar*: drink was served
from the buttery, and drinkers
gathered round the half-door, resting
their tankards on its ledge ('bar').

68   *dry*: thirsty; *and also* 'sexually
inactive' (a moist palm was said to be a
sign of sexual arousal).
69–70   *I am not ... dry*: an allusion to
the proverbial saying 'Fools have wit
enough to keep themselves out of the
rain'.
73   *at my fingers' ends*: always have
a ready supply of jokes; *and* 'have "dry
jests" (i.e. Sir Andrew's fingers) in my
own'.
75   *thou lack'st ... canary*: you need
a drink: 'canary' was a sweet white
wine from the Canary Islands.

Maria
Fare you well, gentlemen.
   Sir Toby
An' thou let part so, Sir Andrew, would thou
might'st never draw sword again!
   Sir Andrew
60 An' you part so, mistress, I would I might never
draw sword again. Fair lady, do you think you have
fools in hand?
   Maria
Sir, I have not you by th' hand.
   Sir Andrew
Marry, but you shall have, and here's my hand.
   Maria
65 Now, sir, thought is free. I pray you bring your
hand to th' buttery bar and let it drink.
   Sir Andrew
Wherefore, sweetheart? What's your metaphor?
   Maria
It's dry, sir.
   Sir Andrew
Why, I think so: I am not such an ass but I can keep
70 my hand dry. But what's your jest?
   Maria
A dry jest, sir.
   Sir Andrew
Are you full of them?
   Maria
Ay, sir, I have them at my fingers' ends: marry, now
I let go your hand, I am barren.   [*Exit* Maria
   Sir Toby
75 O knight, thou lack'st a cup of canary: when did I
see thee so put down?
   Sir Andrew
Never in your life, I think, unless you see canary
put me down. Methinks sometimes I have no more
wit than a Christian or an ordinary man has: but I
80 am a great eater of beef, and I believe that does
harm to my wit.
   Sir Toby
No question.
   Sir Andrew
An' I thought that, I'd forswear it. I'll ride home

76   *put down*: defeated (i.e. by Maria's wit).

78   *put me down*: knock me down (i.e. drunk).

78–9   'Sometimes I think I have no more intelligence than any other Christian man.'

79–81   It was a common belief that because beef is a heavy meat it would dull the brains of those who ate very much: 'beef-witted' meant 'stupid'.

82   *No question*: no doubt about that.

83   *An*: if.
      forswear: give it up.

85   *Pourquoi*: why; but French is obviously not one of the 'three or four languages' that Sir Andrew was said to speak (line 24).

87   *tongues*: languages.

90–3   *Sir Toby puns on 'tongues' (= languages) and 'tongs' (for curling hair); he also glances at a topic often discussed by intellectual Elizabethans—the relationship between 'art' and 'nature'.*

94   *becomes me*: suits me.

95–7   Sir Toby's words are complicated in their meanings and associations. He compares Sir Andrew's hair to the pale yellow fibre *flax*, which was wound on to a cleft stick and then spun off to make linen. Sir Toby expects to see Sir Andrew used as such a *distaff* by a *housewife* in her normal spinning method. But the word 'housewife' was also given to a prostitute—who by taking Sir Andrew *between her legs* would infect him with syphilis and cause his hair to fall out.

98   *I'll home*: I will go home.

99–100   *she'll none of me*: she will not be interested in me.

100   *hard by*: very near here.

103   *estate*: wealth.

104   *there's life in't*: from the proverb 'While there's life, there's hope'.

to-morrow, Sir Toby.

Sir Toby

85 *Pourquoi*, my dear knight?

Sir Andrew

What is '*pourquoi*'? Do, or not do? I would I had bestowed that time in the tongues that I have in fencing, dancing, and bear-baiting. O, had I but followed the arts!

Sir Toby

90 Then hadst thou had an excellent head of hair.

Sir Andrew

Why, would that have mended my hair?

Sir Toby

Past question, for thou seest it will not curl by nature.

Sir Andrew

But it becomes me well enough, does't not?

Sir Toby

95 Excellent, it hangs like flax on a distaff; and I hope to see a housewife take thee between her legs, and spin it off.

Sir Andrew

Faith, I'll home tomorrow, Sir Toby; your niece will not be seen, or if she be, it's four to one she'll

100 none of me: the Count himself here hard by woos her.

Sir Toby

She'll none o' th' Count; she'll not match above her degree, neither in estate, years, nor wit: I have heard her swear't. Tut, there's life in't, man.

106   *masques*: masquerades.

108   *kickshawses*: trifles (from the French *quelque chose*).

109–10   *under . . . betters*: as long as they are not better than I am—i.e. my social superiors

111   *old*: more experienced.

112   *What is thy excellence*: how good are you.
    galliard: a lively dance with five steps, of which the fifth was a little leap in the air.

113   *cut a caper*: perform the leap in the galliard.

114   *mutton*: Sir Toby picks up another sense of 'caper' (= a berry which is used in pickle as sauce for mutton).

115   *back-trick*: probably the innocent Sir Andrew means some kind of reverse step in dancing; but there is a suggestion of sexual ability as he boasts of a *strong* back-trick.

118   *a curtain before 'em*: curtains were hung in front of pictures to protect them from dust and excessive light—or simply to hide them.

119   *Mistress Mall*: this may be a topical allusion (e.g. to Mistress Mary [Mall] Fitton, who was the subject of some court scandal).

121   *coranto*: fast, skipping dance.
    jig: lively, jumping dance.
    make water: urinate.

122   *sink-a-pace*: cinquepace—a five-step dance similar to the galliard; Sir Toby also makes use of 'sink' = sewer.

125   Sir Andrew must have been born when the stars favoured dancing.

126   *does indifferent well*: looks well enough.

127   *dun-coloured stock*: plain brown stocking. Because the first edition (Folio) of this play is not clear at this point, some modern texts read 'flame coloured stock'.

128–29   *born under Taurus*: born at the time when Taurus—the Bull—was the influential sign in the Zodiac (see p. 49). Different astrologers related signs to the various parts of the body.

Sir Andrew

105 I'll stay a month longer. I am a fellow o' th' strangest mind i' th' world: I delight in masques and revels sometimes altogether.

Sir Toby

Art thou good at these kickshawses, knight?

Sir Andrew

As any man in Illyria, whatsoever he be, under the

110 degree of my betters; and yet I will not compare with an old man.

Sir Toby

What is thy excellence in a galliard, knight?

Sir Andrew

Faith, I can cut a caper.

Sir Toby

And I can cut the mutton to't.

Sir Andrew

115 And I think I have the back-trick simply as strong as any man in Illyria.

Sir Toby

Wherefore are these things hid? Wherefore have these gifts a curtain before 'em? Are they like to take dust, like Mistress Mall's picture? Why dost

120 thou not go to church in a galliard, and come home in a coranto? My very walk should be a jig; I would not so much as make water but in a sink-a-pace. What dost thou mean? Is it a world to hide virtues in? I did think, by the excellent constitution of thy

125 leg, it was formed under the star of a galliard.

Sir Andrew

Ay, 'tis strong, and it does indifferent well in a dun-coloured stock. Shall we set about some revels?

Sir Toby

What shall we do else? Were we not born under Taurus?

Sir Andrew

130 Taurus? That's sides and heart.

Sir Toby

No, sir, it is legs and thighs. Let me see thee caper. Ha, higher! Ha, ha, excellent!   [*Exeunt*

Act I   Scene 4
Viola (disguised as a boy and calling herself 'Cesario') has obtained service with Orsino, and has already earned her master's favour. Orsino has confided in her, telling the whole story of his love for Olivia. Now he sends his new page to woo his mistress. But Viola herself has fallen in love!

5   *humour*: nature, temperament.

11   *On your attendance*: I attend on you.
12   *aloof*: aside.
13   *no less but all*: absolutely everything.
    unclasp'd: unlocked; valuable books were often fitted with locks.

15   *address thy gait*: direct your steps.
17   *fixed*: firmly set (as though planted).
18   *audience*: attention.
21   *leap all civil bounds*: go beyond the limits of normal courtesy.
22   *make unprofited return*: come back unsuccessful.
23   *Say I do speak*: suppose that I do speak.
24   *unfold*: tell everything about.
25   *Surprise*: suddenly attack and capture (her heart).

Scene 4 *The* Duke's *court*

Enter Valentine *and* Viola *dressed like a man*

Valentine
If the Duke continue these favours towards you,
Cesario, you are like to be much advanced: he hath
known you but three days, and already you are no
stranger.
Viola
5 You either fear his humour, or my negligence, that
you call in question the continuance of his love. Is
he inconstant, sir, in his favours?
Valentine
No, believe me.

Enter Orsino, Curio, *and Attendants*

Viola
I thank you. Here comes the Count.
Orsino
10 Who saw Cesario, ho?
Viola
On your attendance, my lord, here.
Orsino
[*To* Curio *and Attendants*] Stand you awhile aloof.
[*To* Viola] Cesario,
Thou know'st no less but all: I have unclasp'd
To thee the book even of my secret soul.
15 Therefore, good youth, address thy gait unto her,
Be not denied access, stand at her doors,
And tell them, there thy fixed foot shall grow
Till thou have audience.
Viola   Sure, my noble lord,
If she be so abandon'd to her sorrow
20 As it is spoke, she never will admit me.
Orsino
Be clamorous, and leap all civil bounds,
Rather than make unprofited return.
Viola
Say I do speak with her, my lord, what then?
Orsino
O then unfold the passion of my love,
25 Surprise her with discourse of my dear faith;

28   *nuncio*: messenger.
      aspect: appearance (the stress is
on the second syllable).
30   *belie*: misrepresent.
31   *Diana's lip*: the reference is to
the virgin goddess of chastity.
32   *rubious*: ruby-red; the word
seems to be Shakespeare's own
creation.
      pipe: voice.
33   *organ*: speech organ, voice.
      shrill and sound: high-pitched
and clear.
34   *semblative*: like; this word also
seems to be one of Shakespeare's
coinages.
      part: nature—or theatrical
'character'.
35   *constellation*: personality and
destiny (as ordained by the stars).
      right apt: absolutely right.
38   *When least in company*: i.e.
alone.
41   *a barful strife*: a task full of
obstacles (bars).

It shall become thee well to act my woes:
She will attend it better in thy youth,
Than in a nuncio's of more grave aspect.

        Viola
I think not so, my lord.
        Orsino   Dear lad, believe it—
30 For they shall yet belie thy happy years,
That say thou art a man: Diana's lip
Is not more smooth and rubious; thy small pipe
Is as the maiden's organ, shrill and sound;
And all is semblative a woman's part.
35 I know thy constellation is right apt
For this affair. Some four or five attend him—
All, if you will: for I myself am best
When least in company. Prosper well in this,
And thou shalt live as freely as thy lord,
40 To call his fortunes thine.
        Viola
                    I'll do my best
To woo your lady. [*Aside*] Yet, a barful strife!
Whoe'er I woo, myself would be his wife. [*Exeunt*

Act 1   Scene 5
Maria is scolding Feste for his absence
when Olivia, attended by her steward
Malvolio, enters. Olivia is depressed,
and Feste—the professional jester—
tries to tease her out of her sadness.
But Malvolio is not amused. When he
sneers at the fool, however, Olivia is
quick to defend Feste. Maria
announces the arrival of Orsino's
messenger, but before Viola/Cesario
appears there is an interruption from
the drunken Sir Toby. Viola at last
gains entrance to Olivia's presence
(although Malvolio has tried to prevent
this), and speaks eloquently of Orsino's
love. But Olivia finds the messenger
most attractive; refusing to hear
Orsino's pleas, she sends Malvolio with
a ring to give to 'Cesario'.
3   *in way of thy excuse*: to make
excuses for you.

Scene 5 Olivia's *house*

      Enter Maria *and* Feste

        Maria
Nay, either tell me where thou hast been, or I will
not open my lips so wide as a bristle may enter, in
way of thy excuse. My lady will hang thee for thy
absence.
        Feste
5 Let her hang me: he that is well hanged in this
world needs to fear no colours.
        Maria
Make that good.
        Feste
He shall see none to fear.
        Maria
A good lenten answer. I can tell thee where that
10 saying was born, of 'I fear no colours'.

6   *fear no colours*: fear nothing; this is a military expression (from 'colours' = army banners), and Feste is making a pun on 'colour' and 'collar' (= the hangman's noose).

7   *Make that good*: prove (or explain) that.

9   *lenten*: plain (Lent is the season for fasting).

12–13   *and that ... foolery*: when he is playing the fool for Olivia, Feste can claim that he has been 'in the wars'— i.e. in trouble. Maria's precise meaning is unclear.

14–15   Feste speaks solemn-sounding nonsense—perhaps with overtones of the words from the Bible, 'unto every one that hath shall be given', which occur in the parable of the talents (*Matthew* xxv.29).

17   *turned away*: sacked, dismissed from his post.

20   *let ... out*: may the warm weather of summer make this tolerable.

21   *resolute*: i.e. determined not to answer.

22   *points*: matters; and also (as Maria suggests in the next line) laces fastening together the doublet and breeches.

24   *gaskins*: wide breeches.

27   *piece of Eve's flesh*: i.e. woman— and wife for Sir Toby.

29   *you were best*: it would be best for you.

Feste
Where, good Mistress Mary?

Maria
In the wars, and that may you be bold to say in your foolery.

Feste
Well, God give them wisdom that have it; and those
15 that are fools, let them use their talents.

Maria
Yet you will be hanged for being so long absent; or to be turned away—is not that as good as a hanging to you?

Feste
Many a good hanging prevents a bad marriage and
20 for turning away, let summer bear it out.

Maria
You are resolute then?

Feste
Not so, neither, but I am resolved on two points.

Maria
That if one break, the other will hold: or if both break, your gaskins fall.

Feste
25 Apt, in good faith, very apt. Well, go thy way: if Sir Toby would leave drinking, thou wert as witty a piece of Eve's flesh as any in Illyria.

Maria
Peace, you rogue, no more o' that. Here comes my lady: make your excuse wisely, you were best.

[*Exit*

Enter Olivia, *with* Malvolio *and* Attendants

Feste
30 Wit, an't be thy will, put me into good fooling! Those wits that think they have thee, do very oft prove fools: and I that am sure I lack thee, may pass for a wise man. For what says Quinapalus? 'Better a witty fool than a foolish wit.' God bless
35 thee, lady!

Olivia
Take the fool away.

30   Feste shows his talent in this
invocation: 'wit' (=intelligence,
reason) is usually contrasted with 'will'
(=passion, desire).
    an't: if it.
32–3   *pass for*: be mistaken for.
33   *Quinapalus*: Feste pretends to
quote the words of some great scholar
(whom he has invented), in mockery of
those who try to show their learning in
this way.
38   *Go to*: get away.
    dry: boring; *also* thirsty.
    I'll no more of you: I don't want
to listen to you any more.
39   *dishonest*: disobedient,
unreliable (because he has been away
for so long).
40   *madonna*: my lady; this Italian
word is commonly used to speak of the
Virgin Mary.
42   *mend*: amend *and* repair.
44   *botcher*: a tailor who patches
clothes.
47   *syllogism*: argument.
48   *serve*: be satisfactory.
    so: that's alright.
    what remedy: what can be done
about it.
49–50   More verbal foolery—but
perhaps there is the suggestion that
Olivia will not remain true to her
sorrow (*calamity*), recognizing that her
beauty is like a flower, and will fade as
a flower fades.
53   *Misprision*: misunderstanding.
    in the highest degree: a legal term
meaning 'of the very worst sort'.
53–4   *cucullus ... monachum*: wearing
a monk's cowl (head-covering) does
not make a monk; a proverbial saying.
55   *motley*: a fool's dress.
58   *Dexteriously*: an Elizabethan
form of 'dextrously' (=skilfully).
60   *catechise*: put questions to (a
form of instruction—by question and
answer—used in the Christian church).
60–1   *my mouse*: my little dear (a
common expression of affection).
62   *idleness*: amusement.
    bide: wait for.

Feste
Do you not hear, fellows? Take away the lady.
    Olivia
Go to, y'are a dry fool: I'll no more of you. Besides, you grow dishonest.
    Feste
40 Two faults, madonna, that drink and good counsel will amend: for give the dry fool drink, then is the fool not dry; bid the dishonest man mend himself, if he mend, he is no longer dishonest; if he cannot, let the botcher mend him. Anything that's mended
45 is but patched: virtue that transgresses is but patched with sin, and sin that amends is but patched with virtue. If that this simple syllogism will serve, so: if it will not, what remedy? As there is no true cuckold but calamity, so beauty's a flower.
50 The lady bade take away the fool, therefore I say again, take her away.
    Olivia
Sir, I bade them take away you.
    Feste
Misprision in the highest degree! Lady, *cucullus non facit monachum*: that's as much to say, as I wear
55 not motley in my brain. Good madonna, give me leave to prove you a fool.
    Olivia
Can you do it?
    Feste
Dexteriously, good madonna.
    Olivia
Make your proof.
    Feste
60 I must catechise you for it, madonna. Good my mouse of virtue, answer me.
    Olivia
Well sir, for want of other idleness, I'll bide your proof.
    Feste
Good madonna, why mourn'st thou?
    Olivia
65 Good fool, for my brother's death.
    Feste
I think his soul is in hell, madonna.

Olivia

I know his soul is in heaven, fool.

Feste

The more fool, madonna, to mourn for your brother's soul, being in heaven. Take away the fool,
70 gentlemen.

Olivia

What think you of this fool, Malvolio, doth he not mend?

Malvolio

Yes, and shall do, till the pangs of death shake him. Infirmity, that decays the wise, doth ever make the
75 better fool.

Feste

God send you, sir, a speedy infirmity, for the better increasing your folly! Sir Toby will be sworn that I am no fox, but he will not pass his word for twopence that you are no fool.

Olivia

80 How say you to that, Malvolio?

Malvolio

I marvel your ladyship takes delight in such a barren rascal. I saw him put down the other day with an ordinary fool, that has no more brain than a stone. Look you now, he's out of his guard already!
85 Unless you laugh and minister occasion to him, he is gagged. I protest I take these wise men, that crow so at these set kind of fools, no better than the fools' zanies.

Olivia

O you are sick of self-love, Malvolio, and taste with
90 a distempered appetite. To be generous, guiltless, and of free disposition, is to take those things for bird-bolts that you deem cannon-bullets. There is no slander in an allowed fool, though he do nothing but rail; nor no railing in a known discreet man,
95 though he do nothing but reprove.

Feste

Now Mercury endue thee with leasing, for thou speak'st well of fools!

Enter Maria

---

72   *mend*: improve.

74   *Infirmity*: i.e. the weakness of old age.
  ever: always.
77   *be sworn*: swear.
78   *no fox*: not clever (foxes are remarkably cunning).
78–9   *pass his word ... fool*: not even be bribed—with twopence—to say that Malvolio is not a fool.
82   *barren*: empty (of jokes).
  put down: defeated.
84   *out of his guard*: defenceless— i.e. with nothing to say for himself; the metaphor is from fencing.
85   *minister occasion*: offer opportunity (for jesting).
86   *gagged*: unable to say anything.
  protest: declare.
86–7   *crow so*: laugh so much.
87   *set kind*: professional.
88   *zanies*: stooges, assistants.
90   *distempered*: sick.
91   *of free disposition*: good-natured.
92   *bird-bolts*: short arrows for shooting birds.
  deem: consider.
93–6   The licensed (*allowed*) fool does not slander his victims, even though he does nothing but mock (*rail*) at them; and the man who is known to have good judgement (*known discreet*) is not making mockery (*railing*) even though he does nothing but criticise.
96–7   *Mercury ... fools*: may Mercury (the god of cheating) equip you with skill in lying (*leasing*), since you speak so well of fools (and to do that, one must be able to lie).

Maria

Madam, there is at the gate a young gentleman much desires to speak with you.

Olivia

100 From the Count Orsino, is it?

Maria

I know not, madam: 'tis a fair young man, and well attended.

Olivia

103 *hold him in delay*: are holding him back.

Who of my people hold him in delay?

Maria

Sir Toby, madam, your kinsman.

Olivia

105 Fetch him off, I pray you: he speaks nothing but

106 *madman*: like a madman.

madman. Fie on him!   [*Exit* Maria

107 *suit*: petition.

Go you, Malvolio. If it be a suit from the Count, I am sick, or not at home. What you will, to dismiss it.   [*Exit* Malvolio

110 *old*: stale.

110 Now you see, sir, how your fooling grows old, and people dislike it.

Feste

Thou hast spoke for us, madonna, as if thy eldest son should be a fool: whose skull Jove cram with brains! For here he comes, one of thy kin has a most

115 *pia mater*: brain.

115 weak *pia mater*.

Enter Sir Toby

Olivia

By mine honour, half drunk. What is he at the gate, cousin?

Sir Toby

A gentleman.

Olivia

A gentleman? What gentleman?

Sir Toby

121 *pickle-herring*: Sir Toby pretends that his condition is caused by eating pickled herrings, and not by drink.
  sot: fool; the word also means 'drunkard'.

120 'Tis a gentleman here—[*Belches*] A plague o' these pickle-herring! How now, sot?

Feste

Good Sir Toby!

Olivia.

124 *lethargy*: heavy, drowsy condition; Sir Toby mishears—or pretends to mishear.

Cousin, cousin, how have you come so early by this lethargy?

125   *defy*: despise.

127   *an*: if.
127–8   *give me faith*: i.e. so that he can resist the devil.

131   *draught*: drink.
above heat: that brings his temperature above normal.
132   *mads*: makes him mad.
133   *crowner*: coroner.
133–34   *sit o' my coz*: hold an inquest on my kinsman.

139–40   *takes on him ... much*: he agrees that he knows this.

144   *fortified*: armed and able to resist.

146   *'Has*: he has.
147   *sheriff's post*: decorated posts, the sign of authority, were erected outside the houses of civic officials.
148   *bench*: the preceding 'sheriff's post' leads to a pun with 'bench' = a group of magistrates.
150   *of mankind*: just an ordinary man.

Sir Toby
125   Lechery? I defy lechery. There's one at the gate.
Olivia
Ay, marry, what is he?
Sir Toby
Let him be the devil an he will, I care not: give me faith, say I. Well, it's all one.   [*Exit*
Olivia
What's a drunken man like, fool?
Feste
130   Like a drowned man, a fool, and a madman: one draught above heat makes him a fool, the second mads him, and a third drowns him.
Olivia
Go thou and seek the crowner, and let him sit o' my coz: for he's in the third degree of drink—he's
135   drowned. Go look after him.
Feste
He is but mad yet, madonna, and the fool shall look to the madman.   [*Exit*

Enter Malvolio

Malvolio
Madam, yond young fellow swears he will speak with you. I told him you were sick; he takes on him
140   to understand so much, and therefore comes to speak with you. I told him you were asleep; he seems to have a foreknowledge of that too, and therefore comes to speak with you. What is to be said to him, lady? He's fortified against any denial.
Olivia
145   Tell him, he shall not speak with me.
Malvolio
'Has been told so; and he says he'll stand at your door like a sheriff's post, and be the supporter to a bench, but he'll speak with you.
Olivia
What kind o' man is he?
Malvolio
150   Why, of mankind.
Olivia
What manner of man?

152   *ill manner*: rude.
156   *squash*: unripe peapod (*peascod*).
157   *codling*: unripe apple.
157–58 *in standing water*: at the turn of the tide.
159   *well-favoured*: attractive.
       shrewishly: sharply.

172   *penned*: written (i.e. composed).
       con: learn by heart.
173   *let me ... scorn*: don't laugh at me.
174   *comptible*: sensitive.
       sinister usage: unkindness, discourtesy.
176   *studied*: i.e. as an actor learns his part.
178   *modest*: reasonable.

Malvolio
Of very ill manner: he'll speak with you, will you or no.

Olivia
Of what personage and years is he?

Malvolio
155 Not yet old enough for a man, nor young enough for a boy: as a squash is before 'tis a peascod, or a codling when 'tis almost an apple. 'Tis with him in standing water, between boy and man. He is very well-favoured, and he speaks very shrewishly. One
160 would think his mother's milk were scarce out of him.

Olivia
Let him approach. Call in my gentlewoman.

Malvolio
Gentlewoman, my lady calls.   *[Exit*

Enter Maria

Olivia
Give me my veil: come, throw it o'er my face. We'll
65 once more hear Orsino's embassy.

Enter Viola

Viola
The honourable lady of the house, which is she?

Olivia
Speak to me, I shall answer for her. Your will?

Viola
Most radiant, exquisite, and unmatchable beauty—I pray you tell me if this be the lady of the
170 house, for I never saw her. I would be loath to cast away my speech: for besides that it is excellently well penned, I have taken great pains to con it. Good beauties, let me sustain no scorn; I am very comptible, even to the least sinister usage.

Olivia
175 Whence came you, sir?

Viola
I can say little more than I have studied, and that question's out of my part. Good gentle one, give me modest assurance if you be the lady of the house, that I may proceed in my speech.

180   *comedian*: actor.
181   *my profound heart*: by my most
sincere heart. Some editors interpret
this as an address to Olivia; but I think
it is far too familiar for Viola's present
formal courtesy.
181–82   *by the very fangs of malice*: Viola
swears by all that is cruel (i.e. all the
wicked accusations that could be made
against her). Shakespeare often
associates malice with poisonous
serpents.
182   *I am not that I play*: although
she denies that she is a 'comedian',
Viola admits that she is not what she
appears (i.e. the boy Cesario).
185   *usurp myself*: hold my position
dishonestly.
185–87   Viola argues that Olivia does
hold her position dishonestly because
she should not keep to herself (*reserve*)
that which she ought to give away
(*bestow*).
187   *from my commission*: not in my
instructions.
       I will on: I will go on.
190   *forgive you*: excuse you from.
193   *feigned*: pretended, insincere.
194–95   *allowed your approach*: allowed
you to come in.
197–98   *'tis not . . . dialogue*: I am not at
present in a mood to take part in such a
trivial conversation. (It was believed
that madness was connected with
certain phases of the moon.)
199   *hoist sail*: prepare to leave.
200   *swabber*: deckhand—one who
cleans (swabs) the deck of a ship, as
Maria is attempting to clear Viola from
the room.
       hull: rest (as a ship which lies
with its sails furled).
201   *Some . . . giant*: pacify your
giant. Viola refers to Maria's small
size—and compares her with the giants
who guarded the heroines of popular
romantic fiction.
201–202   *Tell . . . messenger*: Viola is
anxious to hear something from Olivia
that she can report back to Orsino.
204   *when . . . fearful*: when you
begin with such terrifying formality.

Olivia

180 Are you a comedian?

Viola

No, my profound heart: and yet, by the very fangs
of malice, I swear, I am not that I play. Are you the
lady of the house?

Olivia

If I do not usurp myself, I am.

Viola

185 Most certain, if you are she, you do usurp yourself:
for what is yours to bestow is not yours to reserve.
But this is from my commission. I will on with my
speech in your praise, and then show you the heart
of my message.

Olivia

190 Come to what is important in't: I forgive you the
praise.

Viola

Alas, I took great pains to study it, and 'tis poetical.

Olivia

It is the more like to be feigned; I pray you keep it
in. I heard you were saucy at my gates, and allowed
195 your approach rather to wonder at you than to hear
you. If you be mad, be gone: if you have reason, be
brief: 'tis not that time of moon with me to make
one in so skipping a dialogue.

Maria

Will you hoist sail, sir? Here lies your way.

Viola

200 No, good swabber, I am to hull here a little longer.
Some mollification for your giant, sweet lady! Tell
me your mind, I am a messenger.

Olivia

Sure you have some hideous matter to deliver,
when the courtesy of it is so fearful. Speak your
205 office.

Viola

It alone concerns your ear. I bring no overture of
war, no taxation of homage; I hold the olive in my
hand: my words are as full of peace, as matter.

Olivia

Yet you began rudely. What are you? What would
210 you?

205   *office*: business.
206   *overture*: declaration.
207   *taxation of homage*: demand for some kind of payment from a subordinate.
       olive: the olive-branch is a symbol of peace.
208   *my words ... matter*: there is no substance (*matter*) in my words except peace.
212   *entertainment*: reception.
213   *would*: want.
       maidenhead: virginity.
216   *text*: the passage from the Bible upon which a preacher bases his sermon; the preacher begins by declaring the chapter and verse of the book from which the text is taken.
218   *comfortable*: bringing spiritual comfort (a specifically religious term).
220   *bosom*: heart.

Viola
The rudeness that hath appeared in me have I learned from my entertainment. What I am, and what I would, are as secret as maidenhead: to your ears, divinity; to any other's, profanation.

Olivia
215 Give us the place alone: we will hear this divinity.
        [*Exeunt* Maria *and Attendants*
Now, sir, what is your text?

Viola
Most sweet lady—

Olivia
A comfortable doctrine, and much may be said of it. Where lies your text?

Viola
220 In Orsino's bosom.

Olivia

In his bosom? In what chapter of his bosom?

Viola

To answer by the method, in the first of his heart.

Olivia

O, I have read it: it is heresy. Have you no more to say?

Viola

225 Good madam, let me see your face.

Olivia

Have you any commission from your lord to negotiate with my face? You are now out of your text: but we will draw the curtain and show you the picture. [*Removes her veil*] Look you, sir, such a one
230 I was this present. Is't not well done?

Viola

Excellently done, if God did all.

Olivia

'Tis in grain, sir, 'twill endure wind and weather.

Viola

'Tis beauty truly blent, whose red and white
Nature's own sweet and cunning hand laid on.
235 Lady, you are the cruell'st she alive
If you will lead these graces to the grave
And leave the world no copy.

Olivia

O sir, I will not be so hard-hearted: I will give out divers schedules of my beauty. It shall be inven-
240 toried, and every particle and utensil labelled to my will. As *Item*: two lips indifferent red; *Item*: two grey eyes, with lids to them; *Item*: one neck, one chin, and so forth. Were you sent hither to praise me?

Viola

245 I see you what you are, you are too proud:
But if you were the devil, you are fair.
My lord and master loves you: O, such love
Could be but recompens'd, though you were crown'd
The nonpareil of beauty!

Olivia   How does he love me?

Viola

250 With adorations, fertile tears,

---

222   *by the method*: i.e. in the preacher's style—which Olivia and Viola are both using.
223   *heresy*: not a true doctrine.

227–28 *out of your text*: off the subject.

230   *I was this present*: Olivia speaks of her face as though it were a picture recently painted.
231   *if God did all*: i.e. if there are no artificial cosmetics.
232   *in grain*: ingrained, natural.
233   *blent*: blended.
234   *cunning*: skilful.
235   *lead*: carry.
236   *copy*: i.e. a child.

238   *divers*: various.
       schedules: lists of objects for sale, each described individually—as Olivia proceeds to describe her face.
239–40 *every . . . will*: each separate item shall be added on to my will (as normal codicils were pasted on to the main document).
240   *indifferent red*: fairly red.
241   *lids*: eyelids (but intended, in this context, to sound like the lids of saucepans).
242   *praise*: appraise, estimate the value of.
245   *if you were the devil*: even if you were as proud as Lucifer—who was also beautiful when he was an angel.
247   *Could . . . recompens'd*: could never receive more than it deserved.
247–48 *crown'd . . . beauty*: the unequalled queen of beauty.
249   *fertile*: abundant.

252   *suppose him*: believe him to be.
254   *In voices well divulg'd*: well
    spoken of.
        free: generous.
255   *in dimension . . . nature*: in his
    physical form.
256   *gracious*: graceful, attractive.
258   *flame*: spirit.
259   *deadly life*: a life which is dying
    (for the love of Olivia); the *flame* and
    suff'ring make Orsino sound like a
    martyr.
262   *willow*: the emblem of
    disappointed love.
263   *my soul*: i.e. Olivia.
264   *cantons*: songs.
        contemned: rejected.

266   *Halloo*: shout.
        reverberate: resonant.
267   *babbling gossip of the air*: i.e. the
    echo, which is compared to a
    chattering old woman (a *gossip*).
270   *But*: unless.
271   *parentage*: family.
272   *state*: present social rank.

278   *fee'd post*: messenger who
    accepts tips.
280   *Love . . . flint*: may Cupid make
    his heart hard (with the leaden arrow;
    see note to 1.1.35).

With groans that thunder love, with sighs of fire.
    Olivia
Your lord does know my mind, I cannot love him.
Yet I suppose him virtuous, know him noble,
Of great estate, of fresh and stainless youth;
255 In voices well divulg'd, free, learn'd, and valiant,
And in dimension, and the shape of nature,
A gracious person: but yet I cannot love him.
He might have took his answer long ago.
    Viola
If I did love you in my master's flame,
260 With such a suff'ring, such a deadly life,
In your denial I would find no sense,
I would not understand it.
    Olivia   Why, what would you?
    Viola
Make me a willow cabin at your gate,
And call upon my soul within the house;
265 Write loyal cantons of contemned love,
And sing them loud even in the dead of night;
Halloo your name to the reverberate hills,
And make the babbling gossip of the air
Cry out 'Olivia!' O, you should not rest
270 Between the elements of air and earth,
But you should pity me.
    Olivia   You might do much.
What is your parentage?
    Viola
Above my fortunes, yet my state is well:
I am a gentleman.
    Olivia   Get you to your lord:
275 I cannot love him: let him send no more—
Unless, perchance, you come to me again,
To tell me how he takes it. Fare you well.
I thank you for your pains, spend this for me.
    Viola
I am no fee'd post, lady; keep your purse.
280 My master, not myself, lacks recompense.
Love make his heart of flint that you shall love,
And let your fervour like my master's be
Plac'd in contempt. Farewell, fair cruelty.   [*Exit*
    Olivia
'What is your parentage?'

287   *five-fold blazon*: she has just listed five aspects that in themselves form a coat of arms (indicating his noble status).
288   *Unless . . . man*: i.e. if only Orsino were this man.

285   'Above my fortunes, yet my state is well;
       I am a gentleman.' I'll be sworn thou art:
       Thy tongue, thy face, thy limbs, actions, and spirit
       Do give thee five-fold blazon. Not too fast: soft! soft!
       Unless the master were the man—How now?
290   Even so quickly may one catch the plague?
       Methinks I feel this youth's perfections
       With an invisible and subtle stealth
       To creep in at mine eyes. Well, let it be.
       What ho, Malvolio!

                    Enter Malvolio

Malvolio   Here, madam, at your service
Olivia

294   *peevish*: stubborn.
295   *County*: count.
296   *Would I or not*: whether or not I wanted it.
297   *flatter with*: give encouragement to.

295   Run after that same peevish messenger
       The County's man. He left this ring behind him,
       Would I or not. Tell him, I'll none of it;
       Desire him not to flatter with his lord,
       Nor hold him up with hopes: I am not for him.

300   *Hie thee*: hurry.

300   If that the youth will come this way tomorrow,
       I'll give him reasons for't. Hie thee, Malvolio.
Malvolio
       Madam, I will.   [*Exit*
Olivia
       I do I know not what, and fear to find

302–03   *fear . . . mind*: I am afraid that my eye has encouraged my mind (to love).
304   *ourselves we do not owe*: we are not our own masters ('owe' = own, possess).

       Mine eye too great a flatterer for my mind.
305   Fate, show thy force; ourselves we do not owe.
       What is decreed, must be: and be this so.   [*Exit*

Act 2

Act 2   Scene 1
This scene seems to be the parallel of
an earlier one (Act 1 Scene 2). Here is
another sea captain, with a twin who
has been rescued from a shipwreck.
Now it is Sebastian's turn to lament
the loss of his sister, his identical twin,
who must have been drowned.
Sebastian has found a friend in the
captain, Antonio, who accompanies
him despite the personal danger that he
is in.

1–2   *nor . . . you*: and don't you want
me to go with you, either.

3   *By your patience*: be patient
with me.

3–4   *My stars . . . me*: I am an
unlucky person.

4   *malignancy*: bad luck (the evil
influence of his stars).

5   *distemper*: infect.

6   *leave*: permission (with a play
on the meaning 'departure').

10   *sooth*: indeed.
determinate voyage: planned
course of action.

11   *extravagancy*: wandering
around.

11–12   *so . . . modesty*: such good
manners.

12   *extort from me*: force me to tell
you.

13   *what . . . in*: what I want to keep
to myself.

13–14   Because the Captain is too
polite to force information from him,
Sebastian recognizes that common
courtesy demands (*it charges me in
manners*) that he should disclose his
identity (*express myself*).

15   *know of me*: be told by me.

16   *which I called*: I called myself.

Scene 1   *The sea-coast*

Enter Antonio *and* Sebastian

Antonio
Will you stay no longer? Nor will you not that I go
with you?

Sebastian
By your patience, no. My stars shine darkly over
me; the malignancy of my fate might perhaps
5 distemper yours, therefore I shall crave of you your
leave that I may bear my evils alone. It were a bad
recompense for your love, to lay any of them on
you.

Antonio
Let me yet know of you whither you are bound.

Sebastian
10 No, sooth, sir: my determinate voyage is mere
extravagancy. But I perceive in you so excellent a
touch of modesty, that you will not extort from me
what I am willing to keep in; therefore it charges me
in manners the rather to express myself. You must
15 know of me then, Antonio, my name is Sebastian,
which I called Roderigo; my father was that
Sebastian of Messaline whom I know you have
heard of. He left behind him myself and a sister,
both born in an hour; if the heavens had been
20 pleased, would we had so ended! But you, sir,
altered that, for some hour before you took me from
the breach of the sea was my sister drowned.

Antonio
Alas the day!

Sebastian
A lady, sir, though it was said she much resembled
25 me, was yet of many accounted beautiful. But
though I could not with such estimable wonder
overfar believe that, yet thus far I will boldly

17   *Messaline*: a town invented by Shakespeare.
19   *in an hour*: at the same time (i.e. they were twins).
21   *some hour*: about an hour.
22   *breach*: breakers.
25   *was*: who was.
26   *estimable wonder*: wonderful appreciation.
27   *overfar*: too far.
28   *publish her*: describe.
30   *remembrance*: memory.
31   *with more*: i.e. with tears.
32   *your bad entertainment*: the poor hospitality given to you.
33   *your trouble*: for giving you such trouble.
34   *if you will not murder me*: if you don't want to kill me (i.e. by leaving him).
37   *recovered*: saved.
        desire: request.
38   *kindness*: emotion.
39   *yet*: still.
        manners of my mother: the behaviour of a woman.
40–1   *tell tales of me*: betray me (i.e. he will weep).
41   *bound*: going.

publish her: she bore a mind that envy could not but call fair. She is drowned already, sir, with salt water, though I seem to drown her remembrance again with more.

Antonio
Pardon me, sir, your bad entertainment.

Sebastian
O good Antonio, forgive me your trouble.

Antonio
If you will not murder me for my love, let me be your servant.

Sebastian
If you will not undo what you have done—that is, kill him whom you have recovered—desire it not. Fare ye well at once; my bosom is full of kindness, and I am yet so near the manners of my mother that upon the least occasion more mine eyes will tell tales of me. I am bound to the Count Orsino's court. Farewell.   [*Exit*

Antonio
The gentleness of all the gods go with thee!
I have many enemies in Orsino's court,
Else would I very shortly see thee there.
But come what may, I do adore thee so
That danger shall seem sport, and I will go. [*Exit*

Act 2   Scene 2
Malvolio gives Olivia's ring to Viola/Cesario who is bewildered and then realizes the full implications of the situation: Viola loves Orsino; he loves Olivia; she loves Cesario—and Viola/Cesario is one person.

sd   *at several doors*: at different entrances.
1   *ev'n*: just.
2   *on ... pace*: walking reasonably fast.
3   *but hither*: only here.
7   *desperate assurance*: hopeless certainty (i.e. certain that there is no hope).
8   *hardy*: bold.

Scene 2 *A street*

Enter Viola *and* Malvolio, *at several doors*

Malvolio
Were not you ev'n now with the Countess Olivia?

Viola
Even now, sir; on a moderate pace I have since arrived but hither.

Malvolio
She returns this ring to you, sir. You might have saved me my pains, to have taken it away yourself. She adds, moreover, that you should put your lord into a desperate assurance she will none of him. And one thing more, that you be never so hardy to

9–10   *your ... this*: how your lord received this message.
10   *it*: i.e. the ring.
11   *of me*: from me.
13   *stooping for*: picking up. Malvolio has thrown the ring to the ground.
14   *eye*: sight.

17   *outside*: appearance (in male attire).
18   *made good view of*: looked hard at.
20   *in starts*: brokenly, not in complete sentences.
22   *in*: through, by means of.

24   *the man*: i.e. whom she has chosen.

27   *pregnant*: full of ideas.
    enemy: Satan, the 'enemy of mankind' (who is always disguised).
28   *proper false*: handsome deceivers.
29   *waxen*: easily impressed.
    set their forms: imprint themselves (as a seal is imprinted on wax).
30   *the cause*: i.e. of our weakness.
31   'We are what we are made of.'
32   *fadge*: turn out.
33   *monster*: i.e. because both male and female.
    fond: dote.
36   *desperate*: hopeless (appearing as a 'boy', Viola can never hope for Orsino's love).
38   *thriftless*: wasted, unprofitable.

come again in his affairs, unless it be to report your
10 lord's taking of this. Receive it so.
    Viola
She took the ring of me. I'll none of it.
    Malvolio
Come sir, you peevishly threw it to her; and her will
is, it should be so returned. If it be worth stooping
for, there it lies [*throws down the ring*] in your eye;
15 or if not, be it his that finds it.   [*Exit*
    Viola
I left no ring with her: what means this lady?
Fortune forbid my outside have not charm'd her!
She made good view of me, indeed so much
That methought her eyes had lost her tongue,
20 For she did speak in starts, distractedly.
She loves me, sure; the cunning of her passion
Invites me in this churlish messenger.
None of my lord's ring? Why, he sent her none.
I am the man! If it be so, as 'tis,
25 Poor lady, she were better love a dream.
Disguise, I see thou art a wickedness
Wherein the pregnant enemy does much.
How easy is it for the proper false
In women's waxen hearts to set their forms!
30 Alas, our frailty is the cause, not we:
For such as we are made of, such we be.
How will this fadge? My master loves her dearly;
And I, poor monster, fond as much on him;
And she, mistaken, seems to dote on me.
35 What will become of this? As I am man,
My state is desperate for my master's love:
As I am woman (now alas the day!)
What thriftless sighs shall poor Olivia breathe?
O time, thou must untangle this, not I:
40 It is too hard a knot for me t'untie.   [*Exit*

Act 2   Scene 3

Sir Toby and Sir Andrew, in their drunken revelry, are joined by Feste. The singing gets louder, until Maria comes to warn them of Olivia's displeasure. They take no notice, and when Malvolio appears in his official capacity, he includes Maria in the scolding he gives to the revellers, and threatens to report her to her mistress. But Maria has a plan to trick Malvolio and make a fool of him: she will let him find a letter which seems like a declaration of love from Olivia.

2   *betimes*: early.
diluculo surgere: Sir Toby quotes part of a Latin sentence found in all sixteenth-century Latin grammars: *diluculo surgere saluberrimum est*—to rise early is very healthy.
4   *troth*: faith.
6   *conclusion*: reasoning.
can: i.e. drinking vessel.
9–10   *the four elements*: the simple substances of which (it was thought) all matter was compounded: earth, air, fire, and water.
14   *Marian*: he calls for Maria.
stoup: jug.
16   *picture*: the picture (used sometimes as an inn-sign) of two asses entitled 'we three'—the spectator was the third. Feste (the professional fool) jestingly implies that he and the two knights are all asses.
18   *ass*: Sir Toby responds to Feste's joke: the jester has admitted that he himself is an ass.
catch: round, part-song.
19   *breast*: singing-voice.
20–1   'I would give a lot of money to be able to make a bow (*leg*) and sing as sweetly as the fool.' No specific amount is meant by *forty*.
23–4   *Pigrogromitus ... Vapians ... Queubus*: the names are invented; Feste was obviously telling some fantastic traveller's-tale.
25   *leman*: sweetheart.

Scene 3   Olivia's *house*

Enter Sir Toby *and* Sir Andrew

Sir Toby
Approach, Sir Andrew. Not to be abed after midnight, is to be up betimes; and *diluculo surgere*, thou know'st—

Sir Andrew
Nay, by my troth, I know not; but I know, to be up
5 late, is to be up late.

Sir Toby
A false conclusion! I hate it as an unfilled can. To be up after midnight, and to go to bed then, is early; so that to go to bed after midnight is to go to bed betimes. Does not our life consist of the four
10 elements?

Sir Andrew
Faith, so they say; but I think it rather consists of eating and drinking.

Sir Toby
Th'art a scholar; let us therefore eat and drink. Marian, I say! A stoup of wine!

Enter Feste

Sir Andrew
15 Here comes the fool, i' faith.

Feste
How now, my hearts? Did you never see the picture of 'we three'?

Sir Toby
Welcome, ass. Now let's have a catch.

Sir Andrew
By my troth, the fool has an excellent breast. I had
20 rather than forty shillings I had such a leg, and so sweet a breath to sing, as the fool has. In sooth, thou wast in very gracious fooling last night, when thou spok'st of Pigrogromitus, of the Vapians passing the equinoctial of Queubus. 'Twas very good, i'
25 faith. I sent thee sixpence for thy leman: hadst it?

Feste
I did impeticos thy gratillity: for Malvolio's nose is no whipstock, my lady has a white hand, and the Myrmidons are no bottle-ale houses.

26–8   Feste demonstrates the kind of jesting praised by Sir Andrew; there is no special meaning in his words.

26   *impeticos*: put in my petticoat (the jester's professional dress).
        gratillity: gratuity, tip.

27   *whipstock*: whip-handle.

28   *Myrmidons*: followers of the Greek warrior Achilles.

33   *testril*: sixpence.
        a—: there is no reason for this sudden pause; but the position of the word in the Folio text, at the very end of a line of type, suggests that the printer was not paying attention to the sense and missed out the next line of the play.

34   *good life*: Feste means a drinking-song; but Sir Andrew thinks (line 38) that some moral song is suggested.

37   *O mistress mine*: the song is generally appropriate to this play; no particular 'mistress' is intended. (See Appendix, p. 106.)

40   *Trip*: skip.

42   *Every wise-man's son*: every fool; the song refers to the saying that wise men have fools for their sons.

45   *'Tis not hereafter*: it is not something for the future.

47   *still*: always.

48   *plenty*: profit, advantage.

49   *sweet and twenty*: simply a term of endearment (not a reference to the lady's age, or the number of kisses).

51   *mellifluous*: honey-sweet.

52   *contagious breath*: catchy tune; but 'contagious' properly relates to a sickness which is 'catching'.

54   *To hear by the nose*: if we hear the tune with our noses (as we catch the smell of breath).
        dulcet in contagion: sweet in its infection.

Sir Andrew

Excellent! Why, this is the best fooling, when all is
30 done. Now a song!

Sir Toby

Come on, there is sixpence for you. Let's have a
song.

Sir Andrew

There's a testril of me too; if one knight give a—

Feste

Would you have a love-song, or a song of good life?

Sir Toby

35 A love-song, a love-song!

Sir Andrew

Ay, ay. I care not for good life.

Feste

> *O mistress mine, where are you roaming?*
> *O stay and hear, your true love's coming,*
>   *That can sing both high and low.*
40 *Trip no further, pretty sweeting:*
> *Journeys end in lovers meeting,*
>   *Every wise man's son doth know.*

Sir Andrew

Excellent good, i' faith.

Sir Toby

Good, good.

Feste

45 *What is love? 'Tis not hereafter,*
> *Present mirth hath present laughter:*
>   *What's to come is still unsure.*
> *In delay there lies no plenty,*
> *Then come kiss me, sweet and twenty,*
50   *Youth's a stuff will not endure.*

Sir Andrew

A mellifluous voice, as I am a true knight.

Sir Toby

A contagious breath.

Sir Andrew

Very sweet and contagious, i' faith.

Sir Toby

To hear by the nose, it is dulcet in contagion. But

55 *welkin*: skies; Sir Toby suggests that they should drink until the sky seems to spin round.

56 *night-owl*: a bird that wakes at night only, sleeping through the day.

56-7 *draw ... weaver*: a very powerful song. Sir Toby's expression would be comprehensible to an Elizabethan audience familiar with the notions that—
   i. fine music was able to draw a man's soul out of his body.
   ii. man possesses three kinds of soul—vegetable, animal, and rational.
   iii. weavers were usually Puritans and therefore sang only psalms.

58 *An*: if.
   dog: very good.

59 *some dogs*: mechanical devices for gripping.

60 *Thou knave*: there is a round-song of 1609 entitled 'Hold thy peace' where each singer, in turn, addresses the others as 'knave'.

64-5 *Hold thy peace*: be silent.

69 *called up*: sent for.

70 *out of doors*: out of the house.

71 *Cataian*: Chinese (from Cathay), villain; this is more of Sir Toby's nonsense.
   politicians: men of craft and cunning (able to deal with a 'Cataian').

72 *Peg-a-Ramsey*: a character in a popular song.
   Three ... we: a phrase found in several Elizabethan songs.

73 *consanguineous*: of the same blood, related (to Olivia).

74-5 *Tilly-vally ... Lady, Lady*: Sir Toby makes an exclamation of impatience, then scornfully repeats Maria's reference to her 'lady'; and sings the first line of a popular ballad about Susanna and the Elders.

76 *Beshrew me*: a mild oath.

79 *natural*: naturally.

80 Perhaps Sir Toby is misquoting

---

55 shall we make the welkin dance indeed? Shall we rouse the night-owl in a catch that will draw three souls out of one weaver? Shall we do that?

Sir Andrew
An you love me, let's do't: I am dog at a catch.

Feste
By'r lady, sir, and some dogs will catch well.

Sir Andrew
60 Most certain. Let our catch be 'Thou knave'.

Feste
'Hold thy peace, thou knave', knight? I shall be constrained in't to call thee knave, knight.

Sir Andrew
'Tis not the first time I have contrained one to call me knave. Begin, fool [*sings*] it begins; 'Hold thy
65 peace'.

Feste
I shall never begin if I hold my peace.

Sir Andrew
Good, i' faith. Come, begin.
                  [*They join in the singing*

Enter Maria

Maria
What a caterwauling do you keep here? If my lady have not called up her steward Malvolio and bid
70 him turn you out of doors, never trust me.

Sir Toby
My lady's a Cataian, we are politicians, Malvolio's a Peg-a-Ramsey, and [*Sings*] *Three merry men be we.* Am not I consanguineous? Am I not of her blood? Tilly-vally! 'Lady!' [*Sings*] *There dwelt*
75 *a man in Babylon, Lady, Lady.*

Feste
Beshrew me, the knight's in admirable fooling.

Sir Andrew
Ay, he does well enough, if he be disposed, and so do I too: he does it with a better grace, but I do it more natural.

Sir Toby
80   *O' the twelfth day of December—*

Maria
For the love o' God, peace!

the first line of the carol 'The Twelve Days of Christmas'; otherwise the song has not been recognized.

83   *wit*: sense.
       honesty: decency.
86   *coziers*: cobblers.
       mitigation: consideration.
86–7 *remorse of voice*: lowering your voices.

Enter Malvolio

Malvolio
My masters, are you mad? Or what are you? Have you no wit, manners, nor honesty, but to gabble like tinkers at this time of night? Do ye make an ale-
85 house of my lady's house, that ye squeak out your coziers' catches without any mitigation or remorse of voice? Is there no respect of place, persons, nor time in you?

89	*Sneck up*: go away.
90	*round*: blunt.
92	*nothing allied*: not related.
97–107	Sir Toby and Feste sing a song first published in 1600, adapting the words to suit their own situation.
109	*virtuous*: a Puritan; the sect objected to such festivities (*cakes and ale*) as the Twelfth Night celebrations.
111	*Saint Anne*: the mother of the Virgin Mary; a Puritan would find this oath very offensive.
	ginger: used to spice the ale.

Sir Toby
We did keep time, sir, in our catches. Sneck up!

Malvolio
90 Sir Toby, I must be round with you. My lady bade me tell you that, though she harbours you as her kinsman, she's nothing allied to your disorders. If you can separate yourself and your misde-meanours, you are welcome to the house: if not, and 95 it would please you to take leave of her, she is very willing to bid you farewell.

Sir Toby
Farewell, dear heart, since I must needs be gone.

Maria
Nay, good Sir Toby.

Feste
His eyes do show his days are almost done.

Malvolio
100 Is't even so?

Sir Toby
But I will never die.

Feste
Sir Toby, there you lie.

Malvolio
This is much credit to you.

Sir Toby
Shall I bid him go?

Feste
105 *What and if you do?*

Sir Toby
Shall I bid him go, and spare not?

Feste
O no, no, no, no, you dare not.

Sir Toby
Out o' time, sir? ye lie! Art any more than a steward? Dost thou think, because thou art vir-110 tuous, there shall be no more cakes and ale?

Feste
Yes, by Saint Anne, and ginger shall be hot i' th' mouth too.   [*Exit*

Sir Toby
Th'art i' th' right. Go sir, rub your chain with crumbs. A stoup of wine, Maria!

113–14	*rub ... crumbs*: polish your steward's chain (his badge of office)— i.e. remember you are only a servant.

Malvolio

115 Mistress Mary, if you prized my lady's favour at anything more than contempt, you would not give means for this uncivil rule. She shall know of it, by this hand.   [*Exit*

Maria

Go shake your ears.

Sir Andrew

120 'Twere as good a deed as to drink when a man's a-hungry, to challenge him the field and then to break promise with him and make a fool of him.

Sir Toby

Do't, knight. I'll write thee a challenge; or I'll deliver thy indignation to him by word of mouth.

Maria

125 Sweet Sir Toby, be patient for tonight. Since the youth of the Count's was today with my lady, she is much out of quiet. For Monsieur Malvolio, let me alone with him. If I do not gull him into a nayword, and make him a common recreation, do not think I

130 have wit enough to lie straight in my bed. I know I can do it.

Sir Toby

Possess us, possess us, tell us something of him.

Maria

Marry sir, sometimes he is a kind of Puritan.

Sir Andrew

O, if I thought that, I'd beat him like a dog.

Sir Toby

135 What, for being a Puritan? Thy exquisite reason, dear knight?

Sir Andrew

I have no exquisite reason for't, but I have reason good enough.

Maria

The devil a Puritan that he is, or anything const-

140 antly, but a time-pleaser, an affectioned ass that cons state without book, and utters it by great swarths; the best persuaded of himself, so crammed (as he thinks) with excellencies, that it is his grounds of faith that all that look on him love him:

145 and on that vice in him will my revenge find notable cause to work.

---

119   *Go . . . ears*: a common insult, often accompanied with a gesture suggesting that the hearer has the long ears of an ass.

120   *as good . . . drink*: it would be an excellent idea (a common phrase).

121   *the field*: to a duel.

127   *out of quiet*: disturbed.

128   *gull*: play a trick on.
nayword: byword; Maria will fool Malvolio in such a way that his name becomes synonymous with 'fool'.

129   *recreation*: source of amusement.

132   *Possess us*: tell us, let us know your idea.

140   *time-pleaser*: time-server.
affectioned: affected.

141   *cons . . . book*: learns grand language by heart.

141–2   *by great swarths*: in great chunks.

142   *the best persuaded*: with the highest opinion.

144   *grounds of faith*: belief.

150   *expressure of*: expression in.
152   *feelingly personated*: fully
       described.
153   *a forgotten matter*: something
       that we have forgotten.
154   *make distinction of*: tell the
       difference between.
       hands: handwriting.
155   *smell a device*: begin to
       understand the trick.

157   *by*: from.

160   *a horse of that colour*: something
       of that kind (a proverbial expression).

162   *Ass*: Maria puns on 'ass' and
       'as'.

164   *Sport royal*: fun fit for a king.
       physic: medicine.
165–6 *let ... third*: Fabian, not Feste,
       is the third observer in the garden.
167   *construction*: interpretation.
169   *Penthesilea*: queen of the
       warlike race of Amazons; Sir Toby
       praises Maria's wit whilst jesting at her
       size.
170   *Before me*: a mild oath (often
       used instead of 'Before God').

171   *beagle*: small hound.

Sir Toby
What wilt thou do?

Maria
I will drop in his way some obscure epistles of love,
wherein by the colour of his beard, the shape of his
150 leg, the manner of his gait, the expressure of his
eye, forehead, and complexion, he shall find himself most feelingly personated. I can write very like
my lady your niece; on a forgotten matter we can
hardly make distinction of our hands.

Sir Toby
155 Excellent! I smell a device.

Sir Andrew
I have't in my nose too.

Sir Toby
He shall think by the letters that thou wilt drop that
they come from my niece, and that she's in love
with him.

Maria
160 My purpose is indeed a horse of that colour.

Sir Andrew
And your horse now would make him an ass.

Maria
Ass, I doubt not.

Sir Andrew
O, 'twill be admirable!

Maria
Sport royal, I warrant you: I know my physic will
165 work with him. I will plant you two, and let the fool
make a third, where he shall find the letter. Observe
his construction of it. For this night, to bed, and
dream on the event. Farewell.   [*Exit*

Sir Toby
Good night, Penthesilea.

Sir Andrew
170 Before me, she's a good wench.

Sir Toby
She's a beagle, true-bred, and one that adores me—
what o' that?

Sir Andrew
I was adored once too.

Sir Toby
Let's to bed, knight. Thou hadst need send for

176   *recover*: win.
       a foul way out: in a mess (he has
       wasted his money).

178   *cut*: gelding (a castrated horse).

180   *burn*: heat up, with spices.
       sack: a dry white wine.

Act 2   Scene 4
Orsino instructs Viola/Cesario about
the nature of love; and in an oblique
manner Viola confesses her own
feelings. Once again, however, she is
sent to Olivia to court the lady on
behalf of Orsino.

1   *morrow*: morning.
2   *but*: only.
3   *antic*: quaint.
4   *Methought*: I thought.
5   *recollected terms*: elaborate
       musical phrases.

18   *Unstaid*: unsure.
       skittish: playful.
       all motions else: all other
       emotions.

175   more money.

Sir Andrew
If I cannot recover your niece, I am a foul way out.

Sir Toby
Send for money, knight. If thou hast her not i' th'
end, call me cut.

Sir Andrew
If I do not, never trust me, take it how you will.

Sir Toby
180   Come, come, I'll go burn some sack, 'tis too late to
go to bed now. Come, knight; come, knight.

[*Exeunt*

Scene 4   *The* Duke's *court*

Enter Orsino, Viola, Curio, *and others*

Orsino
Give me some music. Now good morrow, friends.
Now, good Cesario, but that piece of song,
That old and antic song we heard last night;
Methought it did relieve my passion much,
5   More than light airs and recollected terms
Of these most brisk and giddy-paced times.
Come, but one verse.

Curio
He is not here, so please your lordship, that should
sing it.

Orsino
10   Who was it?

Curio
Feste the jester, my lord, a fool that the Lady
Olivia's father took much delight in. He is about
the house.

Orsino
Seek him out, and play the tune the while.

[*Exit* Curio. *Music plays*
15   Come hither, boy. If ever thou shalt love,
In the sweet pangs of it remember me.
For such as I am, all true lovers are:
Unstaid and skittish in all motions else

19   *image*: idea.

21–2   The music echoes the very heart of love.

23   *My life upon't*: I would bet my life upon it.

24   *stay'd*: looked, rested.
    favour: face.

25   *by your favour*: if I may say so (with a pun on 'favour' in line 24).

26   *Of your complexion*: rather like you.

29   *still*: always.

30   *wears she to him*: she adapts herself to suit him (as clothes come to fit the wearer).

31   *sways ... heart*: her love holds an equal balance with her husband's.

33   *fancies*: loves.

34   *worn*: exhausted.

37   *hold the bent*: stand the strain. (The 'bent' is the degree to which a bow can be bent before it breaks.)

39   *display'd*: opened, in full bloom.

41   *even*: just.

43   *Mark it*: listen to it.

44   *spinsters*: women spinning thread.

45   *free*: carefree.
    weave ... bones: make lace (using bobbins made of bone).

46   *Do ... it*: often sing it.
    silly sooth: simple truth.

Save in the constant image of the creature
20 That is belov'd. How dost thou like this tune?

Viola
It gives a very echo to the seat
Where love is thron'd.

Orsino   Thou dost speak masterly.
My life upon't, young though thou art, thine eye
Hath stay'd upon some favour that it loves.
25 Hath it not, boy?

Viola   A little, by your favour.

Orsino
What kind of woman is't?

Viola   Of your complexion.

Orsino
She is not worth thee then. What years, i' faith?

Viola
About your years, my lord.

Orsino
Too old, by heaven! Let still the woman take
30 An elder than herself; so wears she to him,
So sways she level in her husband's heart:
For boy, however we do praise ourselves,
Our fancies are more giddy and unfirm,
More longing, wavering, sooner lost and worn
35 Than women's are.

Viola   I think it well, my lord.

Orsino
Then let thy love be younger than thyself,
Or thy affection cannot hold the bent.
For women are as roses, whose fair flower
Being once display'd, doth fall that very hour.

Viola
40 And so they are: alas, that they are so.
To die, even when they to perfection grow!

Enter Curio *and* Feste

Orsino
O, fellow, come, the song we had last night.
Mark it, Cesario—it is old and plain;
The spinsters and the knitters in the sun,
45 And the free maids that weave their threads with bones
Do use to chant it: it is silly sooth,

48   *Like the old age*: as they did in
the old days.
51   *Come away*: come quickly to
me.
52   *cypress*: coffin of cypress wood.
53   *Fie away*: be off.
55   *stuck ... yew*: covered over with
yew-leaves.
57–8   No lover so true ever played my
part, in dying of love.

And dallies with the innocence of love,
Like the old age.
    Feste
Are you ready, sir?
    Orsino
50 Ay, prithee sing.   [*Music*

    Feste
    Come away, come away death,
55 *And in sad cypress let me be laid.*
    Fie away, fie away breath,
    I am slain by a fair cruel maid:
55   *My shroud of white, stuck all with yew,*
            O prepare it.
        My part of death no one so true
            Did share it.

    Not a flower, not a flower sweet,
60 *On my black coffin let there be strewn:*
    Not a friend, not a friend greet
    My poor corpse, where my bones shall be thrown:
        A thousand thousand sighs to save,
            Lay me, O where
65   *Sad true lover never find my grave,*
            To weep there.

    Orsino
There's for thy pains   [*Gives him money*]
    Feste
No pains, sir, I take pleasure in singing, sir.
    Orsino
I'll pay thy pleasure then.
    Feste
70 Truly sir, and pleasure will be paid, one time or
another.
    Orsino
Give me now leave to leave thee.
    Feste
Now the melancholy god protect thee, and the
tailor make thy doublet of changeable taffeta, for
75 thy mind is a very opal. I would have men of such
constancy put to sea, that their business might be
everything, and their intent everywhere, for that's

67   *pains*: troubles (i.e. in singing).
70   *pleasure ... paid*: part of a
proverbial saying that 'pleasure will be
paid for with pain'.
72   The Duke dismisses Feste
politely, speaking as though the fool
were the master.
73   *the melancholy god*: Saturn;
those born under his planet were said
to be of heavy, gloomy temperament.
74–5   Get the tailor to make your next
suit (*doublet*) of shot silk (*taffeta*) which
shows different colours, because you
are always changing your mind.
75   *opal*: a semi-precious stone
which (like taffeta) changes its colour
in different lights.
75ff.   I wish they would make men
like you go to sea (as merchants), so
that they can trade in everything and
sail everywhere, because that's the way
to make a profitable business out of
nothing.

80   *give place*: take themselves away.
81   *yond*: yonder.
     sovereign cruelty: queen of cruelty.
82   *than the world*: than any other in the world.
84   *parts*: property (the 'dirty lands').
85   *hold*: value.
     giddily: lightly (Fortune does not value worldly goods because she is so careless in distributing them).
86   *that ... gems*: i.e. her beauty.
87   *pranks her in*: adorns her with.
89   *Sooth*: indeed.

90   *Say that*: suppose.

97   *retention*: a medical term, referring to the body's ability to retain its contents.
99   *motion*: emotion.
     liver: thought to be the seat of love (cf. 1.1.37); and an organ that helps with digestion.
100 After over-eating (*surfeit*), the appetite is tired of food (cloyed) and rejects it (revolts).

it that always makes a good voyage of nothing. Farewell.   [*Exit*

Orsino
80 Let all the rest give place.
                    [*Exeunt* Curio, *and* Attendants
                         Once more, Cesario,
Get thee to yond same sovereign cruelty.
Tell her my love, more noble than the world,
Prizes not quantity of dirty lands:
The parts that fortune hath bestow'd upon her,
85 Tell her I hold as giddily as fortune.
But 'tis that miracle and queen of gems
That nature pranks her in, attracts my soul.

Viola
But if she cannot love you, sir?

Orsino
I cannot be so answer'd.

Viola   Sooth, but you must.
90 Say that some lady—as perhaps there is—
Hath for your love as great a pang of heart
As you have for Olivia: you cannot love her;
You tell her so. Must she not then be answer'd?

Orsino
There is no woman's sides
95 Can bide the beating of so strong a passion
As love doth give my heart; no woman's heart
So big, to hold so much. They lack retention.
Alas, their love may be call'd appetite,
No motion of the liver, but the palate,
100 That suffers surfeit, cloyment, and revolt;
But mine is all as hungry as the sea,
And can digest as much. Make no compare
Between that love a woman can bear me
And that I owe Olivia.

Viola   Ay, but I know—

Orsino
105 What dost thou know?

Viola
Too well what love women to men may owe.
In faith, they are as true of heart as we.
My father had a daughter lov'd a man—
As it might be, perhaps, were I a woman,
110 I should your lordship.

111   *a blank*: an unwritten book.
112   *concealment*: secrecy.
          worm i'th'bud: i.e. canker, a
disease which destroys roses from the
inside of the flower.
113   *damask*: a blend of red and
white found especially in roses.
          thought: sadness.
114   *with . . . melancholy*: pale and
sick with misery.
115–16   *like . . . grief*: like the smiling
figure of Patience cut on a tombstone.
118   *Our . . . will*: we show greater
passion than we feel.
          still: always.

123   *shall I to*: shall I go to.
          theme: business.
125   *give no place*: not be held back.
          bide no denay: accept no refusal.

Orsino   And what's her history?
Viola
A blank, my lord. She never told her love,
But let concealment, like a worm i' th' bud,
Feed on her damask cheek. She pin'd in thought,
And with a green and yellow melancholy
115   She sat like Patience on a monument,
Smiling at grief. Was not this love indeed?
We men may say more, swear more, but indeed
Our shows are more than will: for still we prove
Much in our vows, but little in our love.
     Orsino
120   But died thy sister of her love, my boy?
     Viola
I am all the daughters of my father's house,
And all the brothers too: and yet I know not.
Sir, shall I to this lady?
     Orsino   Ay, that's the theme.
125   To her in haste; give her this jewel; say
My love can give no place, bide no denay. [*Exeunt*

Act 2   Scene 5
Fabian joins Sir Toby and Sir Andrew
to watch the first part of the trick that
Maria plays on Malvolio. The steward
is already persuaded that Olivia has
some special affection for him, and he
muses aloud—unaware that his words
are overhead. He discovers Maria's
letter and reads that aloud too, unable
at first to understand its meaning.
Finally, overjoyed by his good fortune,
he hurries off to obey certain
instructions in the letter. And the
hidden listeners, with Maria, can enjoy
a good laugh, and the promise of
further amusement.

1   *Come thy ways*: come along.
2   *a scruple*: a very tiny part.
3   *melancholy*: the coldest of the
four humours; Fabian has such a desire
to see this 'sport' that there is more
chance of being 'boiled to death with

Scene 5 Olivia's *garden*

          Enter Sir Toby, Sir Andrew, *and* Fabian
     Sir Toby
Come thy ways, Signior Fabian.
     Fabian
Nay, I'll come. If I lose a scruple of this sport, let
me be boiled to death with melancholy.
     Sir Toby
Would'st thou not be glad to have the niggardly
5   rascally sheep-biter come by some notable shame?
     Fabian
I would exult, man: you know he brought me out o'
favour with my lady about a bear-baiting here.
     Sir Toby
To anger him we'll have the bear again, and we will
fool him black and blue—shall we not, Sir Andrew?

melancholy' than of his being absent from the fun.

5   *sheep-biter*: a mean, sneaking dog that bites the sheep.
     come by: receive.
     shame: disgrace.

7   *a bear-baiting*: the Puritans disapproved of this popular pastime, in which a bear, tethered to a post, was tormented by dogs.

9   *fool him black and blue*: trick Malvolio so that he is badly bruised by their treatment.

11   *An*: if.
      pity of our lives: our lives deserve pity.

11–12   *metal of India*: gold (= 'my precious'); this is one of Sir Toby's terms of affection.

13   *box-tree*: an evergreen shrub, much used for garden-hedges.

15   *practising . . . shadow*: rehearsing gestures, using his shadow as a looking-glass.

15–16   *this half hour*: for the past half hour.

17   *contemplative*: self-deceiving.

20   *tickling*: flattery (as poachers catch trout by tickling them).

22   *she*: i.e. Olivia.
      affect: care for.

23   *fancy*: love.

23–24   *of my complexion*: like me.
         uses: treats.

25   *follows*: serves.

Sir Andrew

10 An' we do not, it is pity of our lives.

Enter Maria.

Sir Toby

Here comes the little villain. How now, my metal of India?

Maria

Get ye all three into the box-tree. Malvolio's coming down this walk; he has been yonder i' the 15 sun practising behaviour to his own shadow this half hour. Observe him, for the love of mockery; for I know this letter will make a contemplative idiot of him. Close, in the name of jesting!
[*The men hide.* Maria *drops a letter*]
Lie thou there, for here comes the trout that must 20 be caught with tickling.   [*Exit*

Enter Malvolio

Malvolio

'Tis but fortune, all is fortune. Maria once told me she did affect me, and I have heard herself come thus near, that should she fancy, it should be one of my complexion. Besides, she uses me with a more 25 exalted respect than any one else that follows her. What should I think on't?

28   *Contemplation*: conceit.
29   *jets*: struts.
     advanced: outspread.

30   '*Slight*: by God's light.

36   *example*: precedent.
36–37   Shakespeare may have invented the story of the *Lady* and the *yeoman of the wardrobe* (= a gentleman's valet); two men with the names Strachy and Yeomans were in fact working in the London theatres at this time—and Yeomans was the wardrobe-keeper.
38   *Jezebel*: the proud wife of King Ahab (*2 Kings* ix. 30ff).
40   *blows*: swells.
42   *state*: chair of state.
43   *stone-bow*: cross-bow which fired stones.
44   *branched*: embroidered (with a design of tree-branches).
45   *day-bed*: couch.

49   *to have … state*: to adopt the grand manner.
50   *demure … regard*: serious look around at those present.
52   *my kinsman Toby*: Malvolio speaks with familiarity, neglecting to say 'Sir Toby'.

Sir Toby
Here's an overweening rogue!

Fabian
O, peace! Contemplation makes a rare turkey-cock of him: how he jets under his advanced plumes!

Sir Andrew
30 'Slight, I could so beat the rogue!

Sir Toby
Peace, I say!

Malvolio
To be Count Malvolio!

Sir Toby
Ah, rogue!

Sir Andrew
Pistol him, pistol him!

Sir Toby
35 Peace, peace!

Malvolio
There is example for't. The Lady of the Strachy married the yeoman of the wardrobe.

Sir Andrew
Fie on him, Jezebel!

Fabian
O peace! Now he's deeply in. Look how imagina-
40 tion blows him.

Malvolio
Having been three months married to her, sitting in my state—

Sir Toby
O for a stone-bow to hit him in the eye!

Malvolio
Calling my officers about me, in my branched
45 velvet gown, having come from a day-bed, where I have left Olivia sleeping—

Sir Toby
Fire and brimstone!

Fabian
O peace, peace!

Malvolio
And then to have the humour of state; and after a
50 demure travel of regard, telling them I know my place, as I would they should do theirs, to ask for my kinsman Toby.

53	*Bolts and shackles*: fetters.

Sir Toby
Bolts and shackles!
Fabian
O peace, peace, peace! Now, now!
Malvolio

55	*start*:
55–6	*make out for*: go off to find.
56	*the while*: during the meantime.
57	*my*—: Malvolio is about to say 'my chain of office', and then he remembers that he will no longer be a steward.
58	*curtsies*: bows low.

55 Seven of my people with an obedient start make out
for him. I frown the while, and perchance wind up
my watch, or play with my [*Touching his chain*]—
some rich jewel. Toby approaches; curtsies there to
me—
Sir Toby
60 Shall this fellow live?
Fabian

61	*cars*: chariots (i.e. 'even if we are torn apart by horse-drawn chariots, we must keep silent').

Though our silence be drawn from us with cars, yet
peace!
Malvolio

64	*austere . . . control*: stern look of authority.
65	*take*: give.

I extend my hand to him thus, quenching my
familiar smile with a austere regard of control—
Sir Toby
65 And does not Toby take you a blow o' the lips then?
Malvolio
Saying, 'Cousin Toby, my fortunes having cast me
on your niece give me this prerogative of speech'.
Sir Toby
What, what?
Malvolio
'You must amend your drunkenness.'
Sir Toby

70	*scab*: a term of abuse.

70 Out, scab!
Fabian

71	*break the sinews*: cut the hamstrings, disable.

Nay, patience, or we break the sinews of our plot.
Malvolio

72	*treasure of your time*: your valuable time.

'Besides, you waste the treasure of your time with a
foolish knight.'
Sir Andrew
That's me, I warrant you.
Malvolio
75 'One Sir Andrew.'
Sir Andrew
I knew 'twas I, for many do call me fool.
Malvolio

77	*employment*: business.

[*Seeing the letter*] What employment have we here?

78   *woodcock . . . gin*: the woodcock was a proverbially foolish bird which was snared in gin-traps.

79–80   *the spirit . . . him*: may he be inspired to read it aloud.

82   *hand*: handwriting.

81–4   Sir Andrew does not appreciate the bawdy joke as Malvolio picks out the C's, the U's, and the T's—spelling 'cut', a slang word for the female genitals. The joke in 'great P's' (=urinates) is obvious when the words are spoken aloud.

83   *great*: capital.

83–4   *in . . . question*: beyond all doubt.

87   *Soft*: gently.

88   *impressure*: seal.
   her Lucrece: i.e. her seal-ring carries the picture of Lucretia, a Roman lady famous for chastity who stabbed herself after she had been raped by Tarquin.

89   *uses to seal*: usually seals her letters.

90   *liver and all*: to the seat of his passion.

95–6   *The numbers altered*: the verse form changed.

98   *brock*: badger (noted for its smell).

100   *Lucrece knife*: the knife that killed Lucretia (see note to 2.5.88).

103   *fustian*: ridiculous.

104   *wench*: i.e. Maria.

107   *dressed*: prepared for.

Fabian

Now is the woodcock near the gin.

Sir Toby

O peace! And the spirit of humours intimate
80 reading aloud to him!

Malvolio

[*Picking up the letter*] By my life, this is my lady's hand: these be her very C's, her U's, and her T's, and thus makes she her great P's. It is in contempt of question her hand.

Sir Andrew

85 Her C's, her U's, and her T's: why that?

Malvolio

[*Reads*] *To the unknown beloved, this, and my good wishes.* Her very phrases! By your leave, wax. Soft! and the impressure her Lucrece, with which she uses to seal. 'Tis my lady! To whom should this be?

[*He opens the letter*

Fabian

90 This wins him, liver and all.

Malvolio

[*Reads*]   *Jove knows I love;*
                   But who?
                   Lips, do not move,
                   No man must know.

95 'No man must know'! What follows? The numbers altered! 'No man must know'! If this should be thee, Malvolio!

Sir Toby

Marry, hang thee, brock!

[*Reads*]   *I may command where I adore;*
100   *But silence, like a Lucrece knife,*
                   With bloodless stroke my heart doth gore;
                   M.O.A.I. doth sway my life.

Fabian

A fustian riddle!

Sir Toby

Excellent wench, say I.

Malvolio

105 '*M.O.A.I. doth sway my life.*'—Nay, but first let me see, let me see, let me see.

Fabian

What dish o' poison has she dressed him!

108   'Just look how the poor hawk (*staniel*) swoops on to it.'

111   *formal capacity*: reasonable mind.
112   *obstruction*: problem.
113   *position*: arrangement.
115   *O ay*: Sir Toby repeats Malvolio's 'O.A.'.
       make up: complete.
       at a cold scent: at a point where the hounds cannot recognize the smell of the animal they are hunting.
116–17   He will think that he has got the truth, even though the deceit is obvious.
116   *Sowter*: a common name for a hound.
       cry upon't: give tongue (a hunting expression, used when the hounds recognize the scent of the hunted animal).
116–117   *as rank ... fox*: stank like a fox (*not* the animal being hunted).
119   *cur*: worthless dog.
120   *faults*: cold scents (the poor hound always claims to have picked up the scent when it is still cold).
121–22   'There is no consistency (*consonancy*) in what follows (*the sequel*).'
122   'That fails (*suffers*) when it is put to the test (*under probation*).'
124   'O' shall end: i.e. he will cry 'O' in shame.
125   *cudgel*: beat.
126   *behind*: at the end.
127   *an*: if.
128   *detraction ... heels*: bad luck following you.
130   *simulation*: puzzle (disguised letters).
131   *crush*: force.
       bow: point.
134   *revolve*: reflect, consider.
       stars: fortune.
137–38   *open their hands*: make a generous offer.

Sir Toby
And with what wing the staniel checks at it!
     Malvolio
'I may command where I adore.' Why, she may
110 command me: I serve her, she is my lady. Why, this
is evident to any formal capacity. There is no
obstruction in this. And the end: what should that
alphabetical position portend? If I could make that
resemble something in me! Softly! 'M.O.A.I.'—
     Sir Toby
115 O ay, make up that! He is now at a cold scent.
     Fabian
Sowter will cry upon't for all this, though it be as
rank as a fox.
     Malvolio
'M'—Malvolio! 'M'! Why, that begins my name!
     Fabian
Did not I say he would work it out? the cur is
120 excellent at faults.
     Malvolio
'M'—But then there is no consonancy in the
sequel; that suffers under probation: 'A' should
follow, but 'O' does.
     Fabian
And 'O' shall end, I hope.
     Sir Toby
125 Ay, or I'll cudgel him, and make him cry 'O'!
     Malvolio
And then 'I' comes behind.
     Fabian
Ay, an' you had any eye behind you, you might see
more detraction at your heels than fortunes before
you.
     Malvolio
130 'M.O.A.I.' This simulation is not as the former:
and yet, to crush this a little, it would bow to me, for
every one of these letters are in my name. Soft!
Here follows prose.   [*Reads*
     If this fall into thy hand, revolve. In my stars I am
135   *above thee, but be not afraid of greatness. Some are*
     born great, some achieve greatness, and some have
     greatness thrust upon 'em. Thy fates open their

The Zodiac

138   *blood and spirit*: spirited courage.
138–39 *to inure thyself*: to get accustomed.
139   *like*: likely.
139–40 *cast ... slough*: throw off your humility as a snake casts off ('sloughs') its old skin.
140   *opposite*: disagreeable.
141–42 *tang ... state*: speak out on important subjects.
142   *trick*: affectation.
143   *singularity*: eccentricity.
145   *ever*: always.
        cross-gartered: garters crossing round the leg and fastening in a bow above the knee (see illustration p. 64).
146   *Go to*: come on.
        thou art made: your fortune is made.
147   *still*: always.
149–50 *alter services*: so that Malvolio became master (cf. 5.1.325).
151   *champaign*: open country.
        discovers: reveals.
152   *open*: unmistakeable.
        politic authors: political books.
153   *baffle*: treat with contempt (technically, 'baffle' = 'to degrade from knighthood').
        wash off: cast off.
        gross acquaintance: any knowledge of common things or people.
154   *point-device*: precisely.
155   *jade*: deceive.
156   *every reason excites*: every argument persuades.
157   *of late*: recently.
160   *injunction*: command.
        habits: clothes.
161   *strange*: distant, aloof.
        stout: proud.
162–63 *even ... on*: as quickly as I can get them on.
165–66 *thou entertain'st*: you accept.
167   *become*: suit.
168   *still*: always.
172   *the Sophy*: the Shah of Persia (who was very generous to two English brothers who visited Persia in 1599).

hands, let thy blood and spirit embrace them; and to inure thyself to what thou art like to be, cast thy
140   humble slough, and appear fresh. Be opposite with a kinsman, surly with servants. Let thy tongue tang arguments of state. Put thyself into the trick of singularity. She thus advises thee, that sighs for thee. Remember who commended thy yellow stock-
145   ings, and wished to see thee ever cross-gartered. I say, remember. Go to, thou art made—if thou desir'st to be so. If not, let me see thee a steward still, the fellow of servants, and not worthy to touch Fortune's fingers. Farewell. She that would alter
150   services with thee,

                    The Fortunate Unhappy.

Daylight and champaign discovers not more! This is open. I will be proud, I will read politic authors, I will baffle Sir Toby, I will wash off gross acquain- tance, I will be point-device the very man. I do not
155   now fool myself, to let imagination jade me; for every reason excites to this, that my lady loves me. She did commend my yellow stockings of late, she did praise my leg being cross-gartered; and in this she manifests herself to my love, and with a kind of
160   injunction drives me to these habits of her liking. I thank my stars, I am happy! I will be strange, stout, in yellow stockings, and cross-gartered, even with the swiftness of putting on. Jove and my stars be praised!—Here is yet a postscript.   [*Reads*
165   *Thou canst not choose but know who I am. If thou entertain'st my love, let it appear in thy smiling; thy smiles become thee well. Therefore in my presence still smile, dear my sweet, I prithee.*
Jove, I thank thee! I will smile, I will do every
170   thing that thou wilt have me.

                                        [*Exit*

Fabian
I will not give my part of this sport for a pension of thousands to be paid from the Sophy.
Sir Toby
I could marry this wench for this device.
Sir Andrew
So could I too.

Sir Toby

175 And ask no other dowry with her but such another jest.

Enter Maria

Sir Andrew

Nor I neither.

Fabian

Here comes my noble gull-catcher.

Sir Toby

Wilt thou set thy foot o' my neck?

Sir Andrew

180 Or o' mine either?

Sir Toby

Shall I play my freedom at tray-trip, and become thy bond-slave?

Sir Andrew

I' faith, or I either?

Sir Toby

Why, thou hast put him in such a dream, that when
185 the image of it leaves him he must run mad.

Maria

Nay, but say true, does it work upon him?

Sir Toby

Like aqua-vitae with a midwife.

Maria

If you will then see the fruits of the sport, mark his
first approach before my lady: he will come to her in
190 yellow stockings, and 'tis a colour she abhors; and
cross-gartered, a fashion she detests; and he will
smile upon her, which will now be so unsuitable to
195 her disposition, being addicted to a melancholy as
she is, that it cannot but turn him into a notable
195 contempt. If you will see it, follow me.

Sir Toby

To the gates of Tartar, thou most excellent devil of wit!

Sir Andrew

I'll make one too.   [*Exeunt*

178   *gull-catcher*: fool-catcher.

179   *set ... neck*: conquerors were usually depicted with one foot on the captive's neck.

181   *play*: gamble.
tray-trip: a dice-game where a player had to throw a three to win.

187   *aqua-vitae*: spirits (alcoholic).

194–95   *notable contempt*: famous disgrace.

196   *Tartar*: Tartarus—hell.

198   *make one*: join the party.

52

Act 3

Act 3   Scene 1
On the way to Olivia's house,
Viola/Cesario meets Feste and engages
in a brief battle of wits with the jester;
she next encounters the two knights,
and at last Olivia appears. Dismissing
the rest of the company, Olivia speaks
to the youth with whom she is in love.

sd   *tabor*: small drum; the stage-
clown usually played on a tabor and a
pipe.

1   *Save*: God save.
3   *live by*: earn a living with.
4   *churchman*: priest.
5   *by*: near.
8   *lies by*: sleeps with.
9   *stands by*: is maintained by.
11   *You have said*: just as you say.
       To ... age: what an age we live
    in.

Scene 1 Olivia's *garden*

> *Enter* Viola, *and* Feste, *who plays on his*
> *pipe and tabor*

Viola
Save thee, friend, and thy music! Dost thou live by
thy tabor?

Feste
No, sir, I live by the church.

Viola
Art thou a churchman?

Feste
5 No such matter, sir. I do live by the church, for I do
live at my house, and my house doth stand by the
church.

Viola
So thou mayst say the king lies by a beggar, if a
beggar dwell near him; or the church stands by thy
10 tabor, if thy tabor stand by the church.

Feste
You have said, sir. To see this age! A sentence is but
a chev'ril glove to a good wit—how quickly the
wrong side may be turned outward!

Viola
Nay, that's certain: they that dally nicely with
15 words may quickly make them wanton.

Feste
I would therefore my sister had had no name, sir.

Viola
Why, man?

Feste
Why, sir, her name's a word, and to dally with that
word might make my sister wanton. But indeed,
20 words are very rascals, since bonds disgraced them.

Viola
Thy reason, man?

11–12   'A wise saying (*sentence*) is like a soft glove to a man of intelligence.'

12   *chev'ril*: kid leather.

14   *dally nicely*: play around.

15   *wanton*: disorderly, unchaste.

16   'That's why I wish my sister had not been given a name.'

20–21   *words are ... them*: i.e. a man's word is no longer to be trusted because his *bond* (= written agreement) is preferred.

22   *Troth*: by my truth.

25   *warrant*: believe.

27–8   *in my conscience*: quite honestly.

29   *I would*: I wish.

34   *pilchards*: small herrings.

37   *late*: recently.

38   *the orb*: the earth.

39ff.   'I would be sorry if the fool could not be with your master as often as with my mistress.' (Feste enjoys visiting Orsino; *and* Orsino can be as foolish as Olivia.)

41   *your wisdom*: your wise self.

42   *an*: if.
  pass upon me: make fun of me.
  I'll no more: I won't talk any longer.

43   *Hold ... thee*: here's something for you to spend.

44   *commodity*: consignment, delivery.

46   *troth*: truth.

49   *these*: i.e. coins.

50   *put to use*: invested.

Feste

Troth, sir, I can yield you none without words, and words are grown so false, I am loath to prove reason with them.

Viola

25 I warrant thou art a merry fellow, and car'st for nothing.

Feste

Not so, sir, I do care for something; but in my conscience, sir, I do not care for you: if that be to care for nothing, sir, I would it would make you

30 invisible.

Viola

Art not thou the Lady Olivia's fool?

Feste

No indeed sir, the Lady Olivia has no folly. She will keep no fool, sir, till she be married, and fools are as like husbands as pilchards are to herrings: the

35 husband's the bigger. I am indeed not her fool, but her corrupter of words.

Viola

I saw thee late at the Count Orsino's.

Feste

Foolery, sir, does walk about the orb like the sun: it shines everywhere. I would be sorry, sir, but the

40 fool should be as oft with your master as with my mistress. I think I saw your wisdom there.

Viola

Nay, an' thou pass upon me, I'll no more with thee. Hold, there's expenses for thee.

  [Gives him a coin

Feste

Now Jove, in his next commodity of hair, send thee

45 a beard!

Viola

By my troth, I'll tell thee, I am almost sick for one—[*Aside*] though I would not have it grow on my chin. Is thy lady within?

Feste

Would not a pair of these have bred, sir?

Viola

50 Yes, being kept together, and put to use.

51–2   Feste alludes to the story of Troilus and Cressida, lovers who were introduced to each other by Cressida's uncle, Pandarus, during the Trojan War (Troy was in Phrygia).

54–5   *begging but a beggar*: he was only asking for a beggar—for a 'Cressida' to go with the original coin, his 'Troilus'.

55   *Cressida ... beggar*: in Robert Henryson's poem *The Testament of Cresseid* the heroine becomes a leper and is obliged to beg for her living; this is not part of the original story—which Shakespeare dramatizes in his play *Troilus and Cressida*.

56   *conster*: explain.

57–58   Feste would like to say 'out of my element' (=not my business), but because *the word is overworn* he tries to find an alternative.

57   *welkin*: sky.

58   *element*: sky.
        overworn: over-used, stale.

60   *craves*: requires.

61   *their ... jests*: the mood of the people he is clowning for.

62   *quality*: social status.
        time: occasion.

63   *the haggard ... feather*: the wild hawk, which must swoop down on every small bird; the fool must not neglect any opportunity for a jest.

64   *practice*: skill.

65   *art*: profession.

66   *fit*: appropriate.

67   *folly-fall'n ... wit*: doing something foolish, ruin (*quite taint*) their reputations for wisdom.

70–1   Sir Andrew has remembered some French, and Viola replies in the same language.

70   'God keep you, sir.'

71   'And you also: your servant.'

73   *encounter*: come towards.

74   *trade be to her*: business is with.

75   *bound to*: obliged to; going to.
        list: aim.

77   *Taste*: try.

Feste
I would play Lord Pandarus of Phrygia, sir, to bring a Cressida to this Troilus.
     Viola
I understand you, sir, 'tis well begged.
                              [*Gives him another coin*
     Feste
The matter, I hope, is not great, sir, begging but a
55 beggar: Cressida was a beggar. My lady is within, sir. I will conster to them whence you come; who you are and what you would are out of my welkin— I might say 'element', but the word is overworn.
                                        [*Exit*
     Viola
This fellow is wise enough to play the fool,
60 And to do that well, craves a kind of wit:
He must observe their mood on whom he jests,
The quality of persons, and the time,
And, like the haggard, check at every feather
That comes before his eye. This is a practice
65 As full of labour as a wise man's art:
For folly that he wisely shows is fit;
But wise men, folly-fall'n, quite taint their wit.

Enter Sir Toby *and* Sir Andrew

     Sir Toby
Save you, gentleman.
     Viola
And you, sir.
     Sir Andrew
70 *Dieu vous garde, monsieur.*
     Viola
Et vous aussi: votre serviteur.
     Sir Andrew
I hope, sir, you are, and I am yours.
     Sir Toby
Will you encounter the house? My niece is desirous you should enter, if your trade be to her.
     Viola
75 I am bound to your niece, sir; I mean, she is the list of my voyage.
     Sir Toby
Taste your legs, sir, put them to motion.

78   *understand me*: stand under me.

81   *to go*: to walk.
82   *answer*: obey.
        with gait and entrance: by
walking and going into the house.
83   *prevented*: forestalled.

87   *My matter*: what I have to say.
        hath no voice: cannot be spoken.
88   *pregnant*: receptive.
        vouchsafed: attentive.

90   *ready*: i.e. ready to use—he will
make a note of them for his own use.

92   *hearing*: audience, meeting.

97   *'Twas ... world*: the world has
not been a happy place.
98   Since pretending to be humble
(*lowly feigning*) was considered the way
to pay compliments.
100   *yours*: i.e. your servant; the
lover was always his lady's 'servant'.
        his ... yours: what is his must
necessarily be yours.
102   *For*: as for.
        on: about.
103   *Would they were blanks*: I would
rather they were empty.

Viola
My legs do better understand me, sir, than I
understand what you mean by bidding me taste my
80 legs.
        Sir Toby
I mean, to go, sir, to enter.
        Viola
I will answer you with gait and entrance; but we are
prevented.

Enter Olivia *and* Maria

Most excellent accomplished lady, the heavens rain
85 odours on you!
        Sir Andrew
That youth's a rare courtier: 'rain odours'—well!
        Viola
My matter hath no voice, lady, but to your own
most pregnant and vouchsafed ear.
        Sir Andrew
'Odours', 'pregnant', and 'vouchsafed': I'll get 'em
90 all three all ready.
        Olivia
Let the garden door be shut, and leave me to my
hearing.
            [*Exeunt* Sir Toby, Sir Andrew, *and* Maria
Give me your hand, sir.
        Viola
My duty, madam, and most humble service.
        Olivia
95 What is your name?
        Viola
Cesario is your servant's name, fair princess.
        Olivia
My servant, sir? 'Twas never merry world
Since lowly feigning was call'd compliment:
Y'are servant to the Count Orsino, youth.
        Viola
100 And he is yours, and his must needs be yours:
Your servant's servant is your servant, madam.
        Olivia
For him, I think not on him; for his thoughts,
Would they were blanks, rather than fill'd with me.

104   *whet*: sharpen, excite.
108   *solicit*: present the argument for (as a lawyer presents his case or *suit*).
109   *music from the spheres*: heavenly harmony created (it was thought) by the planets as they moved in their different orbits; it was inaudible to human ears.
110   *Give . . . you*: please let me speak.
111   'After you had bewitched me last time you were here'.
112   *abuse*: deceive, insult.
114   *hard construction*: severe judgement.
115   *that*: i.e. the ring.
116   *none of yours*: was not yours.
117–21   Olivia suggests that Viola must despise her, treating Olivia's *honour* as though it were a bear fastened to a post (*at the stake*) and tormented (*baited*) by cruel dogs (Viola's own thoughts).
118   *unmuzzled*: with no restraints (the muzzle fits round a dog's jaws to prevent it from biting).
119   *receiving*: understanding.
120   *a cypress*: a thin veil, worn by mourners.

122   *degree*: step.
123   *grize*: step ('grize' and 'degree' are synonymous).
         a vulgar proof: a common experience.
125   'In that case (i.e. that her love is hopeless) I must try to smile again.'
129   *upbraids*: reproaches.
131   *is come to harvest*: has ripened to maturity.
132   *like*: likely.
         proper: handsome.
133   *due west*: directly westwards (Olivia dismisses Viola).
         westward ho: the call of boatmen rowing passengers across the Thames.
134   *Grace*: the grace (blessing) of God.
         good disposition: peace of mind.
135   *You'll nothing*: you will send nothing.

Viola
Madam, I come to whet your gentle thoughts
105 On his behalf.
    Olivia   O, by your leave, I pray you!
I bade you never speak again of him;
But would you undertake another suit,
I had rather hear you to solicit that,
Than music from the spheres.
    Viola   Dear lady—
    Olivia
110 Give me leave, beseech you. I did send,
After the last enchantment you did here,
A ring in chase of you. So did I abuse
Myself, my servant, and, I fear me, you.
Under your hard construction must I sit,
115 To force that on you in a shameful cunning
Which you knew none of yours. What might you
    think?
Have you not set mine honour at the stake,
And baited it with all th' unmuzzled thoughts
That tyrannous heart can think? To one of your
    receiving
120 Enough is shown; a cypress, not a bosom,
Hides my heart. So, let me hear you speak.
    Viola
I pity you.
    Olivia   That's a degree to love.
    Viola
No, not a grize: for 'tis a vulgar proof
That very oft we pity enemies.
    Olivia
125 Why then methinks 'tis time to smile again.
O world, how apt the poor are to be proud!
If one should be a prey, how much the better
To fall before the lion than the wolf! [*Clock strikes*
The clock upbraids me with the waste of time.
130 Be not afraid, good youth, I will not have you.
And yet when wit and youth is come to harvest
Your wife is like to reap a proper man.
There lies your way, due west.
    Viola   Then westward ho!
Grace and good disposition attend your ladyship.
135 You'll nothing, madam, to my lord by me?

138 *That ... are*: i.e. that she is forgetting herself.

139 *the same of you*: i.e. that Viola is not what she appears to be.

140 *what I am*: what I appear to be.

141 'I wish you were what I would like you to be.'

143 *I am your fool*: you are making a fool of me.

144 *what a deal*: how much.

145 'When his mouth shows contempt and anger.'

146 *A murd'rous guilt*: the crime of murder; the Elizabethans believed the proverb 'Murder will out'—i.e. will reveal itself.

147 *love ... hid*: love that tries to conceal itself; another Elizabethan saying was 'Love cannot be hid'.
  Love's ... noon: love is as clear as daylight (midday) when it thinks it is most hidden.

149 *maidhood*: maidenhead, virginity.

150 *maugre*: despite.
  thy pride: i.e. the 'contempt and anger' she describes in line 145.

151 *Nor wit nor reason*: neither intelligence nor sense.

152–3 'Do not force yourself to think (*extort thy reasons*) from this argument (*clause*), that because (*For that*) I am courting you, there is no need for you to court me.'

154 *reason thus ... fetter*: answer one argument with another in this way.

158 *no woman has*: i.e. Viola has not promised her love to any woman.
  nor never none: and there will never be any woman.

161 *deplore*: weep out.

162 *move*: persuade.

Olivia

Stay!
I prithee, tell me what thou think'st of me.

Viola

That you do think you are not what you are.

Olivia

If I think so, I think the same of you.

Viola

140 Then think you right; I am not what I am.

Olivia

I would you were as I would have you be.

Viola

Would it be better, madam, than I am?
I wish it might, for now I am your fool

Olivia

[*Aside*] O what a deal of scorn looks beautiful
145 In the contempt and anger of his lip!
A murd'rous guilt shows not itself more soon
Than love that would seem hid. Love's night is
  noon.
Cesario, by the roses of the spring,
By maidhood, honour, truth, and everything,
150 I love thee so that, maugre all thy pride,
Nor wit nor reason can my passion hide.
Do not extort thy reasons from this clause.
For that I woo, thou therefore hast no cause;
But rather reason thus with reason fetter:
155 Love sought is good, but given unsought is better.

Viola

By innocence I swear, and by my youth,
I have one heart, one bosom, and one truth,
And that no woman has; nor never none
Shall mistress be of it, save I alone.
160 And so adieu, good madam; never more
Will I my master's tears to you deplore.

Olivia

Yet come again: for thou perhaps mayst move
That heart which now abhors, to like his love.

[*Exeunt*

Act 3   Scene 2
Sir Andrew has observed the
conversation between Olivia and
Viola/Cesario, although he was not
able to hear what was being said. He is
ready to give up his hopeless quest for
Olivia's love, but Sir Toby coaxes him
to persist in his efforts by challenging
his 'rival' to a duel. Sir Andrew hurries
away to write his letter, and Maria calls
Sir Toby to witness the result that *her*
letter has produced on Malvolio.

1   *jot*: moment.
2   *dear venom*: my sweet poison
(Sir Toby tries to coax Sir Andrew).
3   *yield*: give.
4   *Marry*: indeed.
6   *orchard*: garden.
7   *the while*: at the time.
9   *argument*: proof.
11   *'Slight*: by God's light.
12   *legitimate*: to be right (as in a
court of law).
12–13   'According to both judgment
and reason.'
14   *grand-jurymen*: expert
witnesses; the grand-jury decided
whether a case was worth a proper
trial.
14–15   *before Noah was a sailor*: before
the Flood.
17   *dormouse*: a very small mouse
which sleeps all winter.
18–19   *fire ... liver*: the heart and liver
were thought to be the seats of courage
(as well as of love).
18   *brimstone*: hell-fire.
19   *accosted*: approached (see *note* to
1.3.46).
20–1   *fire-new ... mint*: as brilliant as
newly-minted coins.
21   *banged*: beaten.
22   *looked ... hand*: expected from
you.
        balked: refused.
23   *double ... opportunity*: more
than golden opportunity.
24–6   Sir Andrew has lost the warmth
of Olivia's affection, and is now out in
the cold, where he will remain unless

Scene 2 Olivia's *house*

Enter Sir Toby, Sir Andrew, *and* Fabian

Sir Andrew
No, faith, I'll not stay a jot longer.
Sir Toby
Thy reason, dear venom, give thy reason.
Fabian
You must needs yield your reason, Sir Andrew.
Sir Andrew
Marry, I saw your niece do more favours to the
5 Count's serving-man than ever she bestowed upon
me. I saw't i' th' orchard.
Sir Toby
Did she see thee the while, old boy, tell me that?
Sir Andrew
As plain as I see you now.
Fabian
This was a great argument of love in her toward
10 you.
Sir Andrew
'Slight! Will you make an ass o' me?
Fabian
I will prove it legitimate, sir, upon the oaths of
judgment and reason.
Sir Toby
And they have been grand-jurymen since before
15 Noah was a sailor.
Fabian
She did show favour to the youth in your sight only
to exasperate you, to awake your dormouse valour,
to put fire in your heart, and brimstone in your
liver. You should then have accosted her, and with
20 some excellent jests, fire-new from the mint, you
should have banged the youth into dumbness. This
was looked for at your hand, and this was balked.
The double gilt of this opportunity you let time
wash off, and you are now sailed into the north of
25 my lady's opinion, where you will hang like an
icicle on a Dutchman's beard, unless you do redeem it by some laudable attempt, either of valour
or policy.

he makes some special effort to win
back her esteem.

24   *are now sailed*: have now sailed.
26   *a Dutchman*: Fabian alludes to
the Dutchman William Barents whose
arctic explorations were much talked
about when this play was written.
27   *laudable attempt*: special effort.
27–8   *valour or policy*: bravery or
cunning.
29   *An't*: if it.
29–30   *policy I hate*: I hate intrigue.
30   *I had as lief*: I would as
willingly.
Brownist: a Puritan sect
(founded by Robert Browne in the
16th century).
politician: schemer.
31–32   *build me . . . valour*: I suggest
that you base your hopes of success on
your courage.
34   *take note*: notice.
love-broker: marriage-broker.
39   *curst*: fierce.
41   *invention*: matter.
Taunt . . . ink: insult him as
much as you can in writing.
41–2   *If thou . . . amiss*: if you address
him about three times as 'thou' it
would not be a bad idea.
43   *as many lies*: as many
accusations of lying (an insult that was
certain to provoke a duel).
45–6   *bed of Ware*: a large bed, almost
3 metres square, at an inn in Ware,
Hertfordshire (now in the Victoria and
Albert Museum, London).
45   *set 'em down*: write them down.
about it: get on with it.
46   *gall enough*: plenty of gall (a pun
on 'gall' = 'bitterness' and the oak-gall
from which ink was made).
47   *goose-pen*: pen made from a
goose-feather; the goose is a
proverbially foolish bird.

Sir Andrew
An't be any way, it must be with valour, for policy
30 I hate: I had as lief be a Brownist as a politician.
Sir Toby
Why then, build me thy fortunes upon the basis of
valour. Challenge me the Count's youth to fight
with him; hurt him in eleven places: my niece shall
take note of it; and assure thyself there is no love-
35 broker in the world can more prevail in man's
commendation with woman than report of valour.
Fabian
There is no way but this, Sir Andrew.
Sir Andrew
Will either of you bear me a challenge to him?
Sir Toby
Go, write it in a martial hand. Be curst and brief: it
40 is no matter how witty, so it be eloquent and full of
invention. Taunt him with the licence of ink. If
thou thou'st him some thrice, it shall not be amiss;
and as many lies as will lie in thy sheet of paper,
although the sheet were big enough for the bed of
45 Ware in England, set 'em down. Go, about it. Let
there be gall enough in thy ink, though thou write
with a goose-pen, no matter. About it!

Sir Andrew
Where shall I find you?
Sir Toby
We'll call thee at thy cubiculo. Go!

49   *cubiculo*: bed-chamber.

[*Exit* Sir Andrew

'Though thou write with a goose-pen' (line 47–48)

50	*dear manikin*: precious little man.
51	*dear to him*: i.e. expensive to him.
51–2	*some two thousand strong*: a good two thousand (ducats).
53	*rare*: extraordinary.
55	*by all means stir*: do everything you can to provoke.
56	*wainropes*: cart-ropes.
57	*hale*: drag.
58	*opened*: dissected.
	blood in his liver: the liver was thought to be the source of blood; lack of blood in the liver indicated cowardice.
60	*anatomy*: corpse.
61	*opposite*: opponent.
	visage: face.
62	*presage*: promise.
63	*the youngest ... nine*: the wren is a small brown bird which lays a lot of eggs; the chick to hatch last is the smallest.
64	*desire the spleen*: want a good laugh (the spleen was thought to have several emotional functions, including the control of laughter).
65	*Yond gull*: that idiot.
66	*renegado*: one who deserts his faith.
67–8	*means ... rightly*: hopes to be saved from damnation by believing in Christ.
68–69	*impossible ... grossness*: incredibly foolish remarks (i.e. Maria's letter).
71–2	*like ... church*: like an old-fashioned school-master who (because he has no proper school-building) teaches his classes in the church.
72	*I have ... murderer*: I have followed him around as carefully as though I were going to murder him.
74–5	*smile ... lines*: crease his face with smiling.
75–6	*the new map ... Indies*: a map of the world published by E. Mollineux in 1599; it showed more details of the East Indies than any previous map, and also included the 'rhumb lines' of navigation.

Fabian

50 This is a dear manikin to you, Sir Toby.

Sir Toby

I have been dear to him, lad, some two thousand strong, or so.

Fabian

We shall have a rare letter from him—but you'll not deliver't—

Sir Toby

55 Never trust me then? and by all means stir on the youth to an answer. I think oxen and wainropes cannot hale them together. For Andrew, if he were opened and you find so much blood in his liver as will clog the foot of a flea, I'll eat the rest of th' 60 anatomy.

Fabian

And his opposite, the youth, bears in his visage no great presage of cruelty.

Enter Maria

Sir Toby

Look where the youngest wren of nine comes.

Maria

If you desire the spleen, and will laugh yourselves 65 into stitches, follow me. Yond gull Malvolio is turned heathen, a very renegado; for there is no Christian, that means to be saved by believing rightly, can ever believe such impossible passages of grossness. He's in yellow stockings!

Sir Toby

70 And cross-gartered?

Maria

Most villainous: like a pedant that keeps a school i' th' church. I have dogged him like his murderer. He does obey every point of the letter that I dropped to betray him. He does smile his face into 75 more lines than is in the new map with the aug-mentation of the Indies: you have not seen such a thing as 'tis! I can hardly forbear hurling things at him—I know my lady will strike him. If she do, he'll smile, and take't for a great favour.

Sir Toby

80 Come bring us, bring us where he is.   [*Exeunt*

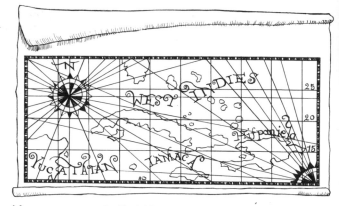

'the new map ... Indies' (Scene 2, lines 75–6)

Act 3   Scene 3

Sebastian and Antonio have now reached the city where Orsino has his court. Sebastian is eager to see the sights, and perhaps even do some shopping, but Antonio dare not accompany him any further. They arrange a time and place to meet and then separate.

1   *by my will*: willingly.
2   *you make ... pains*: you enjoy taking this trouble.
3   *chide*: scold.
4   *stay behind you*: i.e. let you go without me.
5   *filed steel*: i.e. the sharp point of a steel spur.
6   *not all*: it was not only.
6–7   *though ... voyage*: though it was enough to send me on a longer journey.
8   *jealousy*: anxiety.
9   *skilless in*: a stranger in.
12   *The rather*: even more readily.
13   *in your pursuit*: to follow you.
15   *good turns*: kindnesses.
16   *shuffled off*: passed off (not properly repaid).
    uncurrent pay: useless repayment.
17   'If my wealth (*worth*) were as great (*firm*) as my sense (*conscience*) of obligation.'

Scene 3 *The street*

Enter Sebastian *and* Antonio

Sebastian
I would not by my will have troubled you,
But since you make your pleasure of your pains,
I will no further chide you.

Antonio
I could not stay behind you. My desire,
5 More sharp than filed steel, did spur me forth:
And not all love to see you (though so much
As might have drawn one to a longer voyage)
But jealousy what might befall your travel,
Being skilless in these parts: which to a stranger,
10 Unguided and unfriended, often prove
Rough and unhospitable. My willing love
The rather by these arguments of fear
Set forth in your pursuit.

Sebastian   My kind Antonio,
I can no other answer make, but thanks,
15 And thanks, and ever thanks; and oft good turns
Are shuffled off with such uncurrent pay:
But were my worth, as is my conscience, firm,
You should find better dealing. What's to do?
Shall we go see the relics of this town?

Antonio
20 Tomorrow, sir; best first go see your lodging.

18   *dealing*: business.
What's to do?: what shall we do.

19   *relics*: sights, antiquities.

21   *'tis long to night*: there's a long
time before nightfall.

24   *renown*: make famous.
Would . . . me: you'll have to
excuse me.

26   *the Count his*: the Count's.

27   *service*: fighting.
of such note: so considerable.

28   *ta'en*: arrested.
scarce be answer'd: I would have
difficulty in defending myself at a trial.

29   *Belike you slew*: I suppose you
killed.

31   'Although the seriousness of the
occasion and the subject.'

32   *bloody argument*: cause for
bloodshed.

33-5   *It might . . . did*: the quarrel
could have been settled (*answer'd*) by
paying back what we took from them—
and for the sake of trade, most of our
people did that.

35   *stood out*: held out.

36   *lapsed*: arrested.

37   *open*: obviously.

38   *It doth not fit me*: it's not good
for me.

39   *Elephant*: the name of an inn.

40   *bespeak our diet*: order our
meals.

41   *beguile the time*: amuse yourself.

42   *have me*: find me.

43   *Why I your purse?*: why should
I take your money.

44   *Haply*: perhaps.
some toy: some little thing.

45-6   *your store . . . markets*: I don't
think your own money (*store*) is enough
for casual purchases.

47   *purse-bearer*: treasurer.

Sebastian
I am not weary, and 'tis long to night.
I pray you, let us satisfy our eyes
With the memorials and the things of fame
That do renown this city.
    Antonio   Would you'd pardon me:
25 I do not without danger walk these streets.
Once in a sea-fight 'gainst the Count his galleys,
I did some service—of such note indeed,
That were I ta'en here it would scarce be answer'd.
    Sebastian
Belike you slew great number of his people
    Antonio
30 Th' offence is not of such a bloody nature,
Albeit the quality of the time and quarrel
Might well have given us bloody argument.
It might have since been answer'd in repaying
What we took from them, which for traffic's sake
35 Most of our city did. Only myself stood out,
For which, if I be lapsed in this place,
I shall pay dear.
    Sebastian   Do not then walk too open.
    Antonio
It doth not fit me. Hold, sir, here's my purse.
In the south suburbs, at the Elephant,
40 Is best to lodge. I will bespeak our diet
Whiles you beguile the time, and feed your
    knowledge
With viewing of the town. There shall you have me.
    Sebastian
Why I your purse?
    Antonio
Haply your eye shall light upon some toy
45 You have desire to purchase: and your store,
I think, is not for idle markets, sir.
    Sebastian
I'll be your purse-bearer, and leave you for
An hour.
    Antonio
      To th' Elephant.
    Sebastian
             I do remember.
                [Exeunt separately

Act 3   Scene 4

Malvolio appears before Olivia, dressed according to the directions given in Maria's letter and behaving with the familiarity that was recommended there. Olivia is astonished, believing him to be out of his mind; she commits Malvolio to the care of Sir Toby, who treats him as though he were a madman. Sir Andrew brings the challenge that he has written, and Sir Toby (when he has read the letter) promises to deliver it— although he has no such intention. Instead he speaks to Viola/Cesario (who has just parted from Olivia), describing the wrath of Sir Andrew and his skill as a fighter in the most terrifying terms. Returning to Sir Andrew, Sir Toby tells him that his challenge was received with great hostility, and that the youth is determined to fight. Now both duellists are scared, but they are compelled to draw their swords. Suddenly Antonio appears and, mistaking Viola for Sebastian, draws his own sword to fight on his friend's behalf. But the city's officers have been alerted. Antonio is arrested, and he asks for the return of the money that he had given to Sebastian. Of course Viola does not understand, and although she offers money to Antonio she denies any knowledge of him. Deeply hurt by this denial, Antonio is taken to prison and Viola begins to wonder about his mistake.

1	*he says*: if he says.
2	*of*: on.
3	*youth*: the young. Olivia adapts the proverb 'better to buy than to beg or borrow'.
5	*sad and civil*: serious and formal in his behaviour.
9	*possessed*: i.e. by a devil.
12	*were best*: would be advised.

Scene 4 Olivia's *house*

Enter Olivia *and* Maria

Olivia

[*Aside*] I have sent after him, he says he'll come:
How shall I feast him? What bestow of him?
For youth is bought more oft than begg'd or
   borrow'd.
I speak too loud.—
5 Where's Malvolio? He is sad and civil,
And suits well for a servant with my fortunes:
Where is Malvolio?

Maria

He's coming, madam, but in very strange manner.
He is sure possessed, madam.

Olivia

10 Why, what's the matter? Does he rave?

Maria

No, madam, he does nothing but smile: your ladyship were best to have some guard about you if he come, for sure the man is tainted in's wits.

Cross-gartered stockings

Olivia

Go call him hither. [*Exit Maria*] I am as mad as he
15 If sad and merry madness equal be.

Enter Malvolio *with* Maria

How now, Malvolio?

Malvolio

Sweet Lady, ho, ho!

Olivia

Smil'st thou? I sent for thee upon a sad occasion.

Malvolio

Sad, lady? I could be sad: this does make some
20 obstruction in the blood, this cross-gartering; but
what of that? If it please the eye of one, it is with me
as the very true sonnet is: '*Please one, and please all*'.

Olivia

Why, how dost thou, man? What is the matter with
thee?

Malvolio

25 Not black in my mind, though yellow in my legs. It
did come to his hands, and commands shall be
executed. I think we do know the sweet Roman
hand.

18   *upon a sad occasion*: about a serious matter.

22   *sonnet*: song; Malvolio refers to a popular ballad, *Please one, and please all*.

24   *how dost thou*: how are you.

25   *Not ... mind*: not melancholy.
though ... legs: although my legs are yellow (a colour associated with melancholy).

25–6   *It did ... hands*: the letter reached the right man's hands.

27–8   *the sweet Roman hand*: the elegant Italian style of handwriting (which was more fashionable at the time than the traditional English script).

Elizabethan English script

Italian style of handwriting

Olivia

Wilt thou go to bed, Malvolio?

Malvolio

30   To bed? *Ay, sweetheart, and I'll come to thee.*

Olivia

God comfort thee! Why dost thou smile so, and kiss thy hand so oft?

Maria

How do you, Malvolio?

Malvolio

At your request? Yes, nightingales answer daws!

Maria

35   Why appear you with this ridiculous boldness before my lady?

Malvolio

'Be not afraid of greatness': 'twas well writ.

Olivia

What mean'st thou by that, Malvolio?

Malvolio

'Some are born great—'

Olivia

40   Ha?

Malvolio

'Some achieve greatness—'

Olivia

What say'st thou?

Malvolio

'And some have greatness thrust upon them.'

Olivia

Heaven restore thee!

Malvolio

45   'Remember   who   commended   thy   yellow stockings—'

Olivia

Thy yellow stockings?

Malvolio

'And wished to see thee cross-gartered.'

Olivia

Cross-gartered?

Malvolio

50   'Go to, thou art made, if thou desir'st to be so—'

Olivia

Am I made?

---

30   '*Ay, sweetheart ... thee*': a line from a popular song.

34   *At your request*: Malvolio asks Olivia if she wishes him to reply to Maria.
         nightingales: birds with the sweetest song.
         daws: jackdaws (which make an ugly sound).

50–1   *made*: made and mad had the same pronunciation, and Olivia thinks that he is saying she is mad.

Malvolio

'If not, let me see thee a servant still.'

Olivia

Why, this is very midsummer madness.

Enter Servant

Servant

Madam, the young gentleman of the Count
55 Orsino's is returned; I could hardly entreat him
back. He attends your ladyship's pleasure.

Olivia

I'll come to him. [*Exit Servant*] Good Maria, let
this fellow be looked to. Where's my cousin Toby?
Let some of my people have a special care of him; I
60 would not have him miscarry for the half of my
dowry.

[*Exeunt* Olivia *and* Maria *different ways*

Malvolio

O ho, do you come near me now? No worse man
than Sir Toby to look to me! This concurs directly
with the letter: she sends him on purpose, that I
65 may appear stubborn to him; for she incites me to
that in the letter. 'Cast thy humble slough,' says
she; 'be opposite with a kinsman, surly with
servants, let thy tongue tang arguments of state,
put thyself into the trick of singularity'—and con-
70 sequently sets down the manner how: as, a sad face,
a reverend carriage, a slow tongue, in the habit of
some sir of note, and so forth. I have limed her, but
it is Jove's doing, and Jove make me thankful! And
when she went away now, 'Let this fellow be looked
75 to'. 'Fellow'! Not Malvolio, nor after my degree,
but 'fellow'. Why, everything adheres together,
that no dram of a scruple, no scruple of a scruple,
no obstacle, no incredulous or unsafe circumstance—what can be said?—nothing that can
80 be can come between me and the full prospect of
my hopes. Well, Jove, not I, is the doer of this, and
he is to be thanked.

Enter Sir Toby, Fabian, *and* Maria

Sir Toby

Which way is he, in the name of sanctity? If all the

---

53   *midsummer madness*: a proverbial phrase; it was thought that the heat of summer could affect the brain.

55–6   'I could only keep him back with some difficulty (*hardly*).'

60   *miscarry*: come to harm.

62   *do you . . . now*: do you begin to understand me now.
  No worse man: no less.
63   *to look to*: to take care of.
  concurs: agrees.
65   *stubborn*: rude.
69   *consequently*: next.
70   *sets down*: describes.
  sad: serious.
71   *reverend carriage*: dignified deportment.
  in the habit: in the fashion.
72   *some sir of note*: some important personage.
  limed her: caught her—as birds are caught with sticky lime.
74   *fellow*: the usual word referring to a servant; but Malvolio persuades himself that Olivia meant 'my friend', speaking of him as an equal.
75   *after my degree*: as steward.
77   *no dram of a scruple*: not a tiny amount of doubt; a 'dram' is an apothecary's weight for 1/8 ounce.
  no scruple of a scruple: not the least amount of doubt; a 'scruple' is also an apothecary's weight for 1/3 dram.
78   *incredulous*: incredible.
  unsafe: unreliable.
80–1   *full . . . hopes*: fulfilment of all my hopes.

84   *drawn in little*: contracted into his little body.

Legion: the name given to the devil that possessed a madman in St Mark's Gospel, v.8–9.

88   *I discard you*: I want nothing to do with you.

private: privacy.

90   'Listen to the deep (*hollow*) voice of the devil speaking from inside him.'

95   *Let me alone*: leave me to handle him alone.

96   *defy*: renounce.

99   *an*: if.

99–100   *takes it at heart*: becomes distressed.

101   *Carry his water*: take a sample of his urine (for analysis).

th' wise woman: the old woman who could understand and remove the curses of witchcraft.

102–3   *if I live*: as sure as I'm alive.

108   *move*: anger.

110   *rough*: violent.

111–14   *bawcock ... chuck ... biddy*: fine fellow ... chicken ... chickabiddy (terms of endearment spoken to children).

devils of hell be drawn in little, and Legion himself
85 possessed him, yet I'll speak to him.

Fabian
Here he is, here he is. How is't with you, sir? How is't with you, man?

Malvolio
Go off, I discard you. Let me enjoy my private. Go off.

Maria
90 Lo, how hollow the fiend speaks within him! Did not I tell you? Sir Toby, my lady prays you to have a care of him.

Malvolio
[*Aside*] Ah ha! Does she so?

Sir Toby
Go to, go to: peace, peace, we must deal gently with
95 him. Let me alone. How do you, Malvolio? How is't with you? What, man, defy the devil! Consider, he's an enemy to mankind.

Malvolio
Do you know what you say?

Maria
La you, an' you speak ill of the devil, how he takes
100 it at heart! Pray God he be not bewitched!

Fabian
Carry his water to th' wise woman.

Maria
Marry, and it shall be done tomorrow morning, if I live. My lady would not lose him for more than I'll say.

Malvolio
105 How now, mistress?

Maria
O Lord!

Sir Toby
Prithee hold thy peace, this is not the way. Do you not see you move him? Let me alone with him.

Fabian
No way but gentleness, gently, gently: the fiend is
110 rough, and will not be roughly used.

Sir Toby
Why, how now, my bawcock? How dost thou, chuck?

114–15 'tis not ... Satan: it's not right for a sensible man (gravity) to be playing children's games with the devil.

115 cherry-pit: a game of throwing cherry-stones into a hole.

116 foul collier: dirty coalman (coalmen were traditionally associated with the devil because they were dirty and dishonest).

119 minx: shameless woman.

122 I ... element: I do not belong to your world (i.e. he is superior to them).

122–23 know more hereafter: hear more of this later.

125 played: performed.
       could: would.

126 an improbable fiction: something that could never happen.

127 genius: soul.
       taken: caught.

128 device: plot.

129 take air: becomes known, comes into the open.

130 taint: gets spoiled (as milk—for instance—sours when exposed to air).

133 in a dark ... bound: this was the usual treatment for madmen.

135 carry it thus: keep this up, maintain the pretence.

136 pastime: amusement.

137–38 bring ... bar: make it known to everyone (as a prisoner is brought to stand at the barrier—bar—in a public trial).

138–39 crown ... madmen: acknowledge you to be the leader of the jury appointed to decide whether or not the prisoner is insane.

Malvolio
Sir!

Sir Toby
Ay, biddy, come with me. What, man, 'tis not for
115 gravity to play at cherry-pit with Satan. Hang him, foul collier!

Maria
Get him to say his prayers, good Sir Toby, get him to pray.

Malvolio
My prayers, minx!

Maria
120 No, I warrant you, he will not hear of godliness.

Malvolio
Go hang yourselves all. You are idle, shallow things; I am not of your element. You shall know more hereafter.   [*Exit*

Sir Toby
Is't possible?

Fabian
125 If this were played upon a stage now, I could condemn it as an improbable fiction.

Sir Toby
His very genius hath taken the infection of the device, man.

Maria
Nay, pursue him now, lest the device take air, and
130 taint.

Fabian
Why, we shall make him mad indeed.

Maria
The house will be the quieter.

Sir Toby
Come, we'll have him in a dark room and bound. My niece is already in the belief that he's mad: we
135 may carry it thus for our pleasure, and his penance, till our very pastime, tired out of breath, prompt us to have mercy on him; at which time we will bring the device to the bar, and crown thee for a finder of madmen. But see, but see!

Enter Sir Andrew

140   *matter ... morning*: games for a
        holiday (many games and pageants are
        associated with the month of May).
142   *vinegar and pepper in't*: it is
        highly spiced (= insolent).
143   *saucy*: cheeky—with a play on
        'vinegar and pepper'.

146   *whatsoever*: of whatever degree.

149   *admire not*: do not marvel.

151–52 No legal action (*blow of the law*)
        can be taken against Sir Andrew since
        he makes no specific accusation.

154   *uses*: treats.
        thou ... throat: you are a
        complete liar (cf. 3.2.44).

156–57 *sense-less*: the second part of the
        word is '*aside*'—not for Sir Andrew's
        hearing.

159   *chance*: good luck.

162   *o'th' windy side*: to windward,
        on the safe side.

164–65 *my hope is better*: I have a better
        chance of winning.
165–66 *look to*: take care of.
        as thou usest him: if you treat
        him (as a friend).

Fabian
140 More matter for a May morning!
    Sir Andrew
    Here's the challenge, read it: I warrant there's
    vinegar and pepper in't.
    Fabian
    Is't so saucy?
    Sir Andrew
    Ay, is't, I warrant him: do but read.
    Sir Toby
145 Give me. [*Reads*]
    *Youth, whatsoever thou art, thou art but a scurvy
    fellow.*
    Fabian
    Good and valiant
    Sir Toby
    *Wonder not, nor admire not in thy mind, why I do call
150 thee so, for I will show thee no reason for't.*
    Fabian
    A good note; that keeps you from the blow of the
    law.
    Sir Toby
    *Thou com'st to the Lady Olivia, and in my sight she
    uses thee kindly: but thou liest in thy throat; that is
155 not the matter I challenge thee for.*
    Fabian
    Very brief, and to exceeding good sense [*Aside*]-
    less!
    Sir Toby
    *I will waylay thee going home, where if it be thy
    chance to kill me—*
    Fabian
160 Good!
    Sir Toby
    Thou kill'st me like a rogue and a villain.
    Fabian
    Still you keep o' th' windy side of the law: good.
    Sir Toby
    *Fare thee well, and God have mercy upon one of our
    souls! He may have mercy upon mine, but my hope is
165 better, and so look to thyself. Thy friend, as thou usest
    him, and thy sworn enemy,*
        Andrew Aguecheek.

167 *move*: anger; *cannot* picks up another sense of 'move'.

170 *commerce*: conversation

172 *scout me*: keep a look-out.
173 *bum-baily*: bailiff (who comes up behind the man he is arresting).
So: as
174 *draw*: i.e. draw your sword.
175 *comes to pass oft*: often happens.
176 *sharply twanged off*: pronounced boldly.
177 *gives ... approbation*: gives a man greater credit for courage.
proof: being put to the test.
179 *let me alone*: you can't beat me.
181 *gives him out*: shows him.
181–82 *of good ... breeding*: very intelligent and well-educated.
182 *his employment*: the way he is employed (as a messenger).
184 *breed*: give rise to.
185 *find*: realize.
186 *clodpole*: blockhead (literally, one whose head—'poll'—is made from a clod of earth).
187–88 *set ... valour*: tell him that Aguecheek has a remarkable reputation for courage.
189 *aptly receive it*: be quick to understand it.
190 *hideous*: fearful.
192 *cockatrices*: fabulous monsters who were able (it was said) to kill simply by looking at the prey (it is Sir Toby's comic fantasy that a pair of them could kill each other).
193 *give them way*: keep out of their way.
194 *and ... him*: then immediately go after him.
195 *horrid*: terrifying.
198 *laid ... out*: been too extravagant with my honour (i.e. in declaring her love to one whose heart is so hard).

If this letter move him not, his legs cannot. I'll give't him.

Maria
You may have very fit occasion for't. He is now in
170 some commerce with my lady, and will by and by depart.

Sir Toby
Go, Sir Andrew: scout me for him at the corner of the orchard, like a bum-baily. So soon as ever thou see'st him, draw, and as thou draw'st, swear
175 horrible—for it comes to pass oft that a terrible oath, with a swaggering accent sharply twanged off, gives manhood more approbation than ever proof itself would have earned him. Away!

Sir Andrew
Nay, let me alone for swearing.   [*Exit*

Sir Toby
180 Now will not I deliver his letter. For the behaviour of the young gentleman gives him out to be of good capacity and breeding: his employment between his lord and my niece confirms no less. Therefore this letter, being so excellently ignorant, will breed
185 no terror in the youth: he will find it comes from a clodpole. But sir, I will deliver his challenge by word of mouth, set upon Aguecheek a notable report of valour, and drive the gentleman (as I know his youth will aptly receive it) into a most
190 hideous opinion of his rage, skill, fury, and impetuosity. This will so fright them both that they will kill one another by the look, like cockatrices.

Enter Olivia *and* Viola

Fabian
Here he comes with your niece. Give them way till he take leave, and presently after him.

Sir Toby
195 I will meditate the while upon some horrid message for a challenge
              [*Exeunt* Sir Toby, Fabian, *and* Maria

Olivia
I have said too much unto a heart of stone,
And laid mine honour too unchary out.
There's something in me that reproves my fault,

202   *'haviour*: behaviour.
204   *jewel ... picture*: i.e. a miniature portrait of herself, richly framed, to be worn as a pendant.

207–08   'On my honour I shall not refuse anything that you ask, so long as it can be given without loss of honour'.
211   *acquit you*: release you from your promise (i.e. return the love that Olivia has given to Viola, so that it can be given to Orsino).
213   *A fiend like thee*: such an attractive devil as you.
216   *That ... to't*: whatever you have to protect yourself, make use of it.
217   *are thou*: are that thou.
218   *intercepter*: the man who will put an end to your wrong-doing.
    despite: defiance.
    bloody: bloodthirsty; the *hunter* could be either man or dog (hound).
219   *attends*: is lying in wait.
    orchard-end: garden-gate.
219–20   *Dismount thy tuck*: draw your rapier from your belt.
220   *be ... preparation*: get ready quickly (*yare*).
223   *to*: with.
    remembrance: recollection.
224   *image*: memory.
225–26   *if you ... price*: if you value your life at all.
227   *opposite*: opponent.
228   *furnish man withal*: equip a man with.

200   But such a headstrong potent fault it is
That it but mocks reproof.
    Viola
With the same 'haviour that your passion bears
Goes on my master's griefs.
    Olivia
Here, wear this jewel for me, 'tis my picture:
205   Refuse it not, it hath no tongue to vex you.
And I beseech you come again tomorrow.
What shall you ask of me that I'll deny,
That honour sav'd may upon asking give?
    Viola
Nothing but this: your true love for my master.
    Olivia
210   How with mine honour may I give him that
Which I have given to you?
    Viola   I will acquit you.
    Olivia
Well, come again tomorrow. Fare thee well;
A fiend like thee might bear my soul to hell.

                                          [*Exit*

            Enter Sir Toby *and* Fabian

    Sir Toby
Gentleman, God save thee.
    Viola
215   And you, sir.
    Sir Toby
That defence thou hast, betake thee to't. Of what nature the wrongs are thou hast done him, I know not; but thy intercepter, full of despite, bloody as the hunter, attends thee at the orchard-end. Dis-
220   mount thy tuck, be yare in thy preparation, for thy assailant is quick, skilful, and deadly.
    Viola
You mistake, sir; I am sure no man hath any quarrel to me: my remembrance is very free and clear from any image of offence done to any man.
    Sir Toby
225   You'll find it otherwise, I assure you. Therefore, if you hold your life at any price, betake you to your guard; for your opposite hath in him what youth, strength, skill, and wrath, can furnish man withal.

Viola

I pray you sir, what is he?

Sir Toby

230 He is knight dubbed with unhatched rapier, and on
carpet consideration, but he is a devil in private
brawl. Souls and bodies hath he divorced three,
and his incensement at this moment is so implac-
able that satisfaction can be none but by pangs of
235 death and sepulchre. Hob, nob, is his word: give't
or take't.

Viola

I will return again into the house, and desire some
conduct of the lady. I am no fighter. I have heard of
some kind of men that put quarrels purposely on
240 others to taste their valour: belike this is a man of
that quirk.

Sir Toby

Sir, no. His indignation derives itself out of a very
competent injury; therefore get you on, and give
him his desire. Back you shall not to the house,
245 unless you undertake that with me which with as
much safety you might answer him. Therefore on,
or strip your sword stark naked: for meddle you
must, that's certain, or forswear to wear iron about
you.

Viola

250 This is as uncivil as strange. I beseech you, do me
this courteous office, as to know of the knight what
my offence to him is. It is something of my
negligence, nothing of my purpose.

Sir Toby

I will do so. Signior Fabian, stay you by this
255 gentleman till my return.   [*Exit* Sir Toby

Viola

Pray you, sir, do you know of this matter?

Fabian

I know the knight is incensed against you, even to a
mortal arbitrement, but nothing of the circumstance more.

Viola

260 I beseech you, what manner of man is he?

Fabian

Nothing of that wonderful promise, to read him by

230–31   *dubbed . . . consideration*: he was
given his knighthood (*dubbed*) at court
and not on the battlefield (his rapier
had not been hacked—*hatched*—and
there were social—*carpet*—reasons).

232   *Souls . . . three*: i.e. he has killed
three men.

233   *incensement*: rage.

234   *can be none but*: can only be.

235   *sepulchre*: burial
Hob, nob: have or have not
(= come what may).

235–36   *give't or take't*: kill or be killed
('it' is death).

237–38   *desire . . . lady*: ask the lady to
give me an escort.

240   *taste*: test.

241   *quirk*: peculiarity.

242   *derives itself*: is caused by.

241–42   *very competent*: quite adequate.

243   *get you on*: go forward.

244   *his desire*: i.e. a fight.
Back you shall not: you shall not
go back.

245   *that*: i.e. a fight.

246   *answer*: satisfy.

247   *strip . . . naked*: draw your sword
now (and fight with Sir Toby).
meddle: get involved.

248–49   *forswear . . . you*: give up
wearing a sword (i.e. confess that you
are a coward).

250   *uncivil*: incorrect, mistaken.

250–51   *do me . . . office*: be so kind as to
do this for me.

251   *to know of*: to find out from.

252–53   *something . . . negligence*:
something that I have failed to do.

253   *nothing . . . purpose*: I did not
mean to offend him.

258   *a mortal arbitrement*: a fight to
the death to prove his case.
circumstance: details.

261–62   *to read . . . form*: to judge by his
outward appearance.

262   *like*: likely.
262–63   *in the ... valour*: when you put his courage to the test.
264   *bloody*: bloodthirsty.
         fatal: deadly.
         opposite: opponent.
268   *much bound*: greatly indebted.
269   *Sir Priest*: as university graduates, clergymen were given the Latin title *Dominus*; the English equivalent is 'Sir'—the title of a knight.
270   *mettle*: courage.
272   *firago*: Sir Toby's mistaking of 'virago' = a warlike woman.
         pass: fencing bout.
272   *scabbard*: the sheath of the sword; perhaps Sir Toby is imitating the fight—drawing the sword from its sheath; or perhaps he means that Sir Andrew was fighting with the scabbard as well as with his rapier.
273   *gives me the stuck in*: thrusts right into my body.
273–74   *mortal motion*: deadly action.
274   *it is inevitable*: I could not escape.
         on the answer: when the blow is returned.
275   *pays*: stabs, kills.
275–76   'As certainly as your feet touch the ground they stand on.'
276   *Sophy*: Shah of Persia (see *note* to 2.5.172).
277   *Pox on't*: curse it.
280   *Plague on't*: damn it.
         an: if.
281   *cunning in fence*: skilful in fencing.
282–83   *let ... slip*: overlook the matter.
283   *Capilet*: perhaps Shakespeare recalls the name 'Capulet' from his play *Romeo and Juliet*.
284   *motion*: suggestion.
285   *perdition*: loss.
288   *take up*: settle.
290   *He is ... of him*: he (i.e. Viola) is just as frightened of Sir Andrew.
292   *no remedy*: nothing to be done.

his form, as you are like to find him in the proof of his valour. He is indeed, sir, the most skilful, bloody, and fatal opposite that you could possibly
265 have found in any part of Illyria. Will you walk towards him; I will make your peace with him if I can.
        Viola
I shall be much bound to you for't. I am one that had rather go with Sir Priest than Sir Knight: I care
270 not who knows so much of my mettle.   [*Exeunt*

          Enter Sir Toby *and* Sir Andrew
        Sir Toby
Why, man, he's a very devil; I have not seen such a firago. I had a pass with him, rapier, scabbard and all; and he gives me the stuck in with such a mortal motion that it is inevitable. And on the answer, he
275 pays you as surely as your feet hits the ground they step on. They say he has been fencer to the Sophy.
        Sir Andrew
Pox on't, I'll not meddle with him.
        Sir Toby
Ay, but he will not now be pacified: Fabian can scarce hold him yonder.
        Sir Andrew
280 Plague on't, an' I thought he had been valiant, and so cunning in fence, I'd have seen him damned ere I'd have challenged him. Let him let the matter slip, and I'll give him my horse, grey Capilet.
        Sir Toby
I'll make the motion. Stand here, make a good show
285 on't: this shall end without the perdition of souls. [*Aside*] Marry, I'll ride your horse as well as I ride you.

          Enter Fabian *and* Viola
[*To Fabian*] I have his horse to take up the quarrel; I have persuaded him the youth's a devil.
        Fabian
290 He is as horribly conceited of him, and pants and looks pale, as if a bear were at his heels.
        Sir Toby
[*To Viola*] There's no remedy, sir, he will fight with

293   *for's oath sake*: because he has sworn to do so.

293–94   *better . . . quarrel*: thought again about the reason for his quarrel with you.

295–96   *draw . . . vow*: draw your sword so that he can keep his vow (to fight).

296   *protests*: promises.

298–99   *A little . . . them*: it would not take much to make me tell them.

299   *how much . . . man*: what a coward I am (also 'that I am not a man').

300   *Give ground*: yield.

303   *bout*: fencing matches are divided into bouts, where each fighter is allowed a certain number of thrusts.

304   *duello*: code of rules governing the conduct of a duel.

306   *to't*: get on with it.

311   *I for . . . you*: challenge you on his behalf.

315   *undertaker*: one who acts on another's behalf.
       I am for you: I am ready to fight you.

316   *officers*: i.e. the state's policemen.

---

you for's oath sake. Marry, he hath better bethought him of his quarrel, and he finds that now
295 scarce to be worth talking of. Therefore, draw for the supportance of his vow; he protests he will not hurt you.

Viola
[*Aside*] Pray God defend me! A little thing would make me tell them how much I lack of a man.

Fabian
300 [*To Sir Andrew*] Give ground if you see him furious.

Sir Toby
Come, Sir Andrew, there's no remedy; the gentleman will for his honour's sake have one bout with you. He cannot by the duello avoid it, but he has
305 promised me, as he is a gentleman and a soldier, he will not hurt you. Come on, to't.

Sir Andrew
Pray God he keep his oath!

Enter Antonio

Viola
I do assure you, 'tis against my will.
            [Sir Andrew *and* Viola *draw their swords*

Antonio
[*Drawing*] Put up your sword! If this young gentleman
310 Have done offence, I take the fault on me:
If you offend him, I for him defy you.

Sir Toby
You, sir? Why, what are you?

Antonio
One, sir, that for his love dares yet do more
Than you have heard him brag to you he will.

Sir Toby
315 Nay, if you be an undertaker, I am for you.

            [*Draws*

Enter Two Officers

Fabian
O good Sir Toby, hold! Here come the officers.

317   *I'll . . . anon*: I'll see you later (a threat).

318   *put . . . up*: put your sword away.

320   *Marry, will I*: I most certainly will.

      for that: as for that which.

321   *He*: i.e. the horse, 'grey Capilet' (line 283).

322   *reins well*: goes well in a bridle.

323   *office*: duty.

324   *at the suit*: on the authority.

326   *favour*: face.

330   *answer it*: atone for.

Sir Toby
[*To Antonio*] I'll be with you anon.

Viola
[*To Sir Andrew*] Pray sir, put your sword up, if you please.

Sir Andrew
320 Marry, will I, sir: and for that I promised you, I'll be as good as my word. He will bear you easily, and reins well.

First Officer
This is the man; do thy office.

Second Officer
Antonio, I arrest thee at the suit.

325 Of Count Orsino.

Antonio   You do mistake me, sir.

First Officer
No, sir, no jot: I know your favour well,
Though now you have no sea-cap on your head.
Take him away; he knows I know him well.

Antonio
I must obey. [*To Viola*] This comes with seeking you;

330 But there's no remedy, I shall answer it.
What will you do, now my necessity

334 *befalls myself*: happens to me.
amaz'd: bewildered.
335 *be of comfort*: cheer up.

337 *entreat of you*: ask you for.

340 *part*: partly.
341 *lean . . . ability*: very little money.
342 *My . . . much*: I do not have much.
343 'I'll divide what I have at the moment with you.'
344 *coffer*: wealth.
345 *deny*: refuse.
346 *my deserts to you*: what I deserve from you.
347 *lack persuasion*: fail to persuade you.
tempt: provoke.
348 *unsound*: weak (morally weak, because good deeds should be done for their own sakes, not in the hope of reward).
349 *upbraid*: reproach.
353 *vainness*: boasting.
355 *Inhabits . . . blood*: is inherent in weak human nature.

359 *Reliev'd*: took care.
sanctity of love: pure and intense devotion.
360 *image*: appearance.
360–61 *promise . . . worth*: show itself to be worthy of great respect.
361 *did I devotion*: I worshipped.

Makes me to ask you for my purse? It grieves me
Much more for what I cannot do for you,
Than what befalls myself. You stand amaz'd,
335 But be of comfort.

Second Officer
Come, sir, away.

Antonio
I must entreat of you some of that money.

Viola
What money, sir?
For the fair kindness you have show'd me here,
340 And part being prompted by your present trouble,
Out of my lean and low ability
I'll lend you something. My having is not much;
I'll make division of my present with you.
Hold, there's half my coffer.

[*Offers Antonio money*

Antonio
345 Will you deny me now?   [*Refuses it*
Is't possible that my deserts to you
Can lack persuasion? Do not tempt my misery,
Lest that it make me so unsound a man
As to upbraid you with those kindnesses
350 That I have done for you.

Viola   I know of none,
Nor know I you by voice or any feature.
I hate ingratitude more in a man
Than lying, vainness, babbling drunkenness,
Or any taint of vice whose strong corruption
355 Inhabits our frail blood.

Antonio   O heavens themselves!

Second Officer
Come sir, I pray you go.

Antonio
Let me speak a little. This youth that you see here
I snatch'd one half out of the jaws of death,
Reliev'd him with such sanctity of love,
360 And to his image, which methought did promise
Most venerable worth, did I devotion.

First Officer
What's that to us? The time goes by. Away!

Antonio
But O how vile an idol proves this god!

364   *done . . . shame*: abused a good appearance.
366   *unkind*: hard-hearted (and therefore unnatural).
367–68   'The virtuous are beautiful, but those who are beautiful and wicked are merely empty bodies, richly decorated (*o'er-flourish'd*) by the devil.'

373   *so do not I*: I do not believe— i.e. that what she has heard is true, and that her brother has been *snatch'd one half out of the jaws of death* (line 358).
375   *ta'en*: mistaken.
377   *couplet*: Sir Toby derides the rhymed couplets of Viola's speeches.
        sage saws: wise proverbs.
378–79 *I . . . glass*: I see a living image of my brother every time I look in the mirror.
379   *even . . . so*: exactly like this.
380   *favour*: face.
381   *Still . . . fashion*: always in clothes of this style.
384   *dishonest*: dishonourable.
        paltry: contemptible.
385   *hare*: the hare is easily frightened and runs with speed, thus earning a reputation for cowardice.
386   *in necessity*: when he was in need.
        denying him: refusing to recognize him.
387   *cowardship*: cowardice.
388   *devout*: devoted, sincere.
        religious in it: acting as though cowardice were his religion.
389   *'Slid*: by God's eyelid.
        I'll after: I'll go after.
390   *cuff him soundly*: give him a good slap with your hand.
391   *An*: if.
392   *the event*: what will happen.
393   *lay any money*: bet any amount of money.
        yet: after all.

Thou hast, Sebastian, done good feature shame.
365 In nature there's no blemish but the mind:
None can be call'd deform'd but the unkind.
Virtue is beauty, but the beauteous evil
Are empty trunks, o'er-flourish'd by the devil.
    First Officer
The man grows mad, away with him! Come, come,
370 sir.
    Antonio
Lead me on.   [*Exit with* Officers
    Viola
Methinks his words do from such passion fly
That he believes himself; so do not I!
Prove true, imagination, O prove true,
375 That I, dear brother, be now ta'en for you!
    Sir Toby
Come hither, knight, come hither, Fabian. We'll
whisper o'er a couplet or two of most sage saws.
    Viola
He nam'd Sebastian. I my brother know
Yet living in my glass; even such and so
380 In favour was my brother, and he went
Still in this fashion, colour, ornament,
For him I imitate. O if it prove,
Tempests are kind, and salt waves fresh in love!
                                     [*Exit*

    Sir Toby
A very dishonest paltry boy, and more a coward
385 than a hare. His dishonesty appears in leaving his
friend here in necessity, and denying him; and for
his cowardship, ask Fabian.
    Fabian
A coward, a most devout coward, religious in it!
    Sir Andrew
'Slid, I'll after him again, and beat him.
    Sir Toby
390 Do, cuff him soundly, but never draw thy sword.
    Sir Andrew
An' I do not—   [*Exit*
    Fabian
Come, let's see the event.
    Sir Toby
I dare lay any money 'twill be nothing yet. [*Exeunt*

Act 4

Act 4 Scene 1

Feste encounters Sebastian, and of course mistakes him for his twin. The same mistake is made by Sir Andrew and Sir Toby, who attempt to resume the duel that was interrupted by Antonio. Now it is Olivia who intervenes. She invites the youth whom she calls 'Cesario' to come home with her; and Sebastian is delighted to accept.

1   *am not sent*: have not been sent.
3   *Go to*: go away.
4   *clear*: rid.
5   *held out*: kept up (i.e. the pretence of not recognizing Feste).
10   *vent thy folly*: play your silly games.
12   *of*: spoken by.
14–15   *I am . . . cockney*: I think the whole stupid world is going crazy.
14   *lubber*: lout.
15   *prove*: turn out to be.
       cockney: pretentious fop.
15–16   *ungird thy strangeness*: stop being silly—put off (*ungird*) your odd behaviour in pretending not to know me.
16   *vent*: say.
18   *foolish Greek*: silly clown (the term 'merry Greek' was a common expression).
19   *tarry*: stay around.
21   *thou . . . hand*: you are very generous (Feste perhaps remembers an earlier gift—3.1.43).
23   *report*: reputation.
       after . . . purchase: when they have paid an excessive amount for it: *purchase* = the price of a piece of land, which was reckoned to be the equivalent of twelve years' rent.

Scene 1 *The street*

Enter Sebastian *and* Feste

Feste
Will you make me believe that I am not sent for you?

Sebastian
Go to, go to, thou art a foolish fellow, let me be clear of thee.

Feste
5 Well held out, i' faith! No, I do not know you, nor I am not sent to you by my lady, to bid you come speak with her; nor your name is not Master Cesario; nor this is not my nose neither. Nothing that is so, is so.

Sebastian
10 I prithee vent thy folly somewhere else. Thou know'st not me.

Feste
Vent my folly! He has heard that word of some great man, and now applies it to a fool. Vent my folly! I am afraid this great lubber, the world, will
15 prove a cockney. I prithee now, ungird thy strangeness, and tell me what I shall vent to my lady. Shall I vent to her that thou art coming?

Sebastian
I prithee, foolish Greek, depart from me. There's money for thee: if you tarry longer, I shall give
20 worse payment.

Feste
By my troth, thou hast an open hand. These wise men that give fools money get themselves a good report—after fourteen years' purchase.

Enter Sir Andrew, Sir Toby, *and* Fabian

24   *There's for you*: take that (he
strikes Sebastian).

27   *Hold*: stop it.

28   *straight*: at once.
29   *in some of your coats*: in the
situation that some of you are in.
30   *Come on*: come away; Sir Toby
tries to restrain Sebastian.
31   *let*: leave.
31–2   *I'll go ... with him*: I'll get even
with him another way.
32   *action of battery*: charge of
unlawful assault.
        against: brought against.
34   *it's ... that*: that won't make
any difference.

37   *put up your iron*: put your sword
away.
        you ... fleshed: you have had a
good taste of blood.
40   *tempt*: try.

42   *malapert*: impudent.

43   *charge*: command.

45   *Will ... thus*: is it always going
to be like this.
47   *preach'd*: taught.

Sir Andrew
Now sir, have I met you again? There's for you!
                                    [*Strikes* Sebastian
Sebastian
25 Why, there's for thee, and there, and there!
                                    [*Beats* Sir Andrew]
Are all the people mad?
Sir Toby
Hold, sir, or I'll throw your dagger o'er the house.
Feste
This will I tell my lady straight. I would not be in
some of your coats for twopence.   [*Exit*
Sir Toby
30 Come on, sir, hold!
Sir Andrew
Nay, let him alone, I'll go another way to work with
him. I'll have an action of battery against him, if
there be any law in Illyria; though I struck him
first, yet it's no matter for that.
Sebastian
35 Let go thy hand!
Sir Toby
Come, sir, I will not let you go. Come, my young
soldier, put up your iron: you are well fleshed.
Come on!
Sebastian
I will be free from thee. What would'st thou now?
40 If thou dar'st tempt me further, draw thy sword.
                                              [*Draws*
Sir Toby
What, what! Nay, then, I must have an ounce or
two of this malapert blood from you.   [*Draws*

Enter Olivia

Olivia
Hold, Toby! on thy life I charge thee, hold!
Sir Toby
Madam!
Olivia
45 Will it be ever thus? Ungracious wretch,
Fit for the mountains and the barbarous caves
Where manners ne'er were preach'd! Out of my
sight!

Be not offended, dear Cesario.
50   Rudesby, be gone!
            [*Exeunt* Sir Toby, Sir Andrew, *and* Fabian
                              I prithee, gentle friend,
        Let thy fair wisdom, not thy passion, sway
        In this uncivil and unjust extent
        Against thy peace. Go with me to my house,
        And hear thou there how many fruitless pranks

50   *Rudesby*: ruffian.

51   *sway*: rule.
52   *uncivil and unjust*: barbarous
  and unjustified.
        extent: act of violence.
54   *fruitless*: pointless.

55   *botch'd up*: patched together, fooled around with.

    thereby: i.e. hearing of Sir Toby's other stupidities will make this outrage seem just as trivial.

56   *Thou ... go*: you have no choice but to come with me.

57   *deny*: refuse.

    Beshrew: a (mild) curse on.

58   'He frightened my heart when he attacked you.' Olivia alludes to the romantic notion that lovers exchange hearts (so that *her* heart would be in Sebastian's body). As a technical term in hunting, *started* = roused; and its use here allows for a pun with 'heart' and 'hart'.

59   *What ... this*: what does this taste of (i.e. mean).

    How ... stream: what's going on now.

60   *Or ... or ...*: either ... or.

61   *fancy*: imagination.

    still: always.

    sense: reason.

    in Lethe steep: drown in Lethe (the river, in classical mythology, whose waters caused total oblivion).

62   *still*: for ever.

63   *I prithee ... me*: I wish you would do what I suggest.

65   *say so, and so be*: i.e. say you will be ruled (by Olivia), and be so indeed.

---

55 This ruffian hath botch'd up, that thou thereby
May'st smile at this. Thou shalt not choose but go:
Do not deny. Beshrew his soul for me!
He started one poor heart of mine, in thee.

Sebastian
[*Aside*] What relish is in this? How runs the stream?
60 Or I am mad, or else this is a dream:
Let fancy still my sense in Lethe steep;
If it be thus to dream, still let me sleep!

Olivia
Nay, come, I prithee; would thou'dst be rul'd by me!

Sebastian
Madam, I will.

Olivia   O, say so, and so be.   [*Exeunt*

Act 4 Scene 2
Disguised as a parson, Feste torments Malvolio (who has been locked in a dark room) by treating him like a madman. Sir Toby laughs, but he is now ready to put an end to the joke. Feste, this time without his disguise, speaks to Malvolio and agrees to take a letter to Olivia.

1   *gown*: the black gown of the priest and scholar.

Scene 2 Olivia's *house*

Enter Maria *and* Feste

Maria
Nay, I prithee put on this gown, and this beard; make him believe thou art Sir Topas the curate. Do it quickly. I'll call Sir Toby the whilst.   [*Exit*

Feste
Well, I'll put it on, and I will dissemble myself in't;
5 and I would I were the first that ever dissembled in

2   *Sir Topas*: the title 'Sir' was used for priests and scholars (see *note* 3.4.269); 'Sir Topas' is the name of a knight in one of Chaucer's *Canterbury Tales*; and the topaz, a precious stone, was thought to have powers in curing lunacy.

3   *the whilst*: meanwhile.

4   *dissemble*: disguise.

5   *I would*: I wish.
     dissembled: pretended to be something they were not.

6–7   *become ... well*: be really impressive in this role.

8   *student*: scholar (who ought to spend his time and money on books— and would therefore be *lean* (= thin) and hungry-looking).
     said: called.

8–9   *good housekeeper*: hospitable man.

9   *goes as fairly*: is just as suitable.

10   *competitors*: confederates.

12–16   *Bonos dies*: good day. The bad Latin begins Feste's caricature of a 'Master Parson'; he continues in this speech to mock the pedantic forms of speech, and the quoting of authority. The *hermit of Prague* is an invention; *Gorboduc* was a legendary king of Britain; and what follows— '*that that ... is*'? is mock logic without any particular meaning.

18   *Peace in this prison*: the greeting is prescribed in the Elizabethan *Book of Common Prayer* for the priest's entry into a sick-room.

19   *knave*: lad (used with friendly familiarity of servants).

20sd   *Within*: Malvolio does not come on to the stage but speaks from inside the 'dark room' with which he was threatened in 3.4.133.

such a gown. I am not tall enough to become the function well, nor lean enough to be thought a good student. But to be said an honest man and a good housekeeper goes as fairly as to say a careful man and a great scholar. The competitors enter.

Enter Sir Toby *and* Maria

Sir Toby
Jove bless thee, Master Parson.

Feste
Bonos dies, Sir Toby: for as the old hermit of Prague, that never saw pen and ink, very wittily said to a niece of King Gorboduc, 'That that is, is': so I, being Master Parson, am Master Parson; for what is 'that' but 'that'? and 'is' but 'is'?

Sir Toby
To him, Sir Topas.

Feste
What ho, I say! Peace in this prison!

Sir Toby
The knave counterfeits well: a good knave.

Malvolio
[*Within*] Who calls there?

Feste
Sir Topas the curate, who comes to visit Malvolio the lunatic.

Malvolio

Sir Topas, Sir Topas, good Sir Topas, go to my lady!

Feste

25 Out, hyperbolical fiend! How vexest thou this man! Talkest thou nothing but of ladies?

Sir Toby

Well said, Master Parson.

Malvolio

Sir Topas, never was man thus wronged. Good Sir Topas, do not think I am mad. They have laid me 30 here in hideous darkness.

Feste

Fie, thou dishonest Satan! (I call thee by the most modest terms, for I am one of those gentle ones that will use the devil himself with courtesy.) Say'st thou that the house is dark?

Malvolio

35 As hell, Sir Topas.

Feste

Why, it hath bay-windows transparent as barri-cadoes, and the clerestories toward the south-north are as lustrous as ebony: and yet complainest thou of obstruction?

Malvolio

40 I am not mad, Sir Topas. I say to you, this house is dark.

Feste

Madman, thou errest. I say there is no darkness but ignorance, in which thou art more puzzled than the Egyptians in their fog.

Malvolio

45 I say this house is as dark as ignorance, though ignorance were as dark as hell; and I say there was never man thus abused. I am no more mad than you are—make the trial of it in any constant question.

Feste

What is the opinion of Pythagoras concerning 50 wildfowl?

Malvolio

That the soul of our grandam might haply inhabit a bird.

---

25   *Out ... fiend*: Feste addresses the over-powering (*hyperbolical* = exaggerated) devil which—they pretend— has taken possession of Malvolio.

32   *modest*: moderate.
33   *use*: treat.
34   *house*: room.

36   *barricadoes*: barricades (which would shut out any light).
37   *clerestories*: upper windows.
    south-north: an intentionally meaningless direction.
38   *lustrous*: shining.
    ebony: the darkest of all woods.
39   *of obstruction*: that the light is shut out.
43   *puzzled*: lost (i.e. in ignorance).
44   *the Egyptians ... fog*: the plague of darkness which covered Egypt for three days (*Exodus*, x. 21–3).
47   *abused*: badly treated.
48   *make the trial of it*: test my sanity.
    constant question: logical discussion.
49   *Pythagoras*: a Greek philosopher who taught that when a man died, his soul entered into a bird (this was the doctrine of 'the transmigration of the soul').
51   *grandam*: grandmother—i.e. ancestor.
    haply: perhaps.

54   *I think nobly*: Malvolio holds the Christian belief in the immortality of the soul.

57   *hold*: believe.
57–8   *allow of thy wits*: certify that you are sane.
58   *woodcock*: a proverbially foolish bird.
59   *dispossess*: dislodge.

62   *for all waters*: ready for anything.
63–4   This is a reasonable enough comment from the point of view of the characters in the scene; but Feste's disguise certainly improves the comedy for a theatre audience.
65   *To him . . . voice*: now speak to him in your own voice.
66–7   *I . . . knavery*: I wish we could get this joke finished off.
67   *conveniently delivered*: released without much trouble.
68   *would*: wish.
     so far in offence: in so much trouble.
70   *upshot*: conclusion.
72   *Hey Robin . . .*: an Elizabethan popular song.

75   *perdie*: by God (French *par Dieu*).

Feste
What think'st thou of his opinion?
Malvolio
I think nobly of the soul, and no way approve his
55 opinion.
Feste
Fare thee well: remain thou still in darkness. Thou
shalt hold th' opinion of Pythagoras ere I will allow
of thy wits, and fear to kill a woodcock lest thou
dispossess the soul of thy grandam. Fare thee well.
Malvolio
60 Sir Topas, Sir Topas!
Sir Toby
My most exquisite Sir Topas!
Feste
Nay, I am for all waters.
Maria
Thou might'st have done this without thy beard
and gown; he sees thee not.
Sir Toby
65 To him in thine own voice, and bring me word how
thou find'st him. I would we were well rid of this
knavery. If he may be conveniently delivered, I
would he were, for I am now so far in offence with
my niece that I cannot pursue with any safety this
70 sport to the upshot. Come by and by to my
chamber.

[*Exit with* Maria

Feste
   Hey Robin, jolly Robin,
   Tell me how thy lady does.
Malvolio
Fool!
Feste
   My lady is unkind, perdie.
Malvolio
Fool!
Feste
   Alas, why is she so?
Malvolio
Fool, I say!
Feste
   *She loves another—*Who calls, ha?

80–4   *as ever . . . hand*: if you ever want to do something for me which will be well rewarded.

81   *help me to*: fetch me.

82–3   *I will . . . for't*: As long as I live, I shall be grateful to you for this.

86   *how . . . wits*: how did you come to be out of your senses (the *five wits* are the five faculties of the human mind: common wit, imagination, fantasy, judgement, and memory).

87   *notoriously abused*: shamefully ill-treated.

89   *But as well*: only as well (i.e. no better than).

91   *propertied me*: treated me like a senseless object.

93   *to face . . . wits*: to drive me out of my mind.

94   *Advise you*: be careful.

95–6   *thy wits . . . restore*: may the heavens restore you to your right mind.

96–7   *endeavour . . . sleep*: try to get some sleep.

97   *vain bibble babble*: meaningless prattle.

99   *Maintain no words*: don't try to talk.

100–01   *God buy you*: God be with you.

104   *shent*: scolded.

Malvolio

80 Good fool, as ever thou wilt deserve well at my hand, help me to a candle, and pen, ink, and paper. As I am a gentleman, I will live to be thankful to thee for't.

Feste

Master Malvolio?

Malvolio

85 Ay, good fool.

Feste

Alas, sir, how fell you besides your five wits?

Malvolio

Fool, there was never man so notoriously abused! I am as well in my wits, fool, as thou art.

Feste

But as well? Then you are mad indeed, if you be no

90 better in your wits than a fool.

Malvolio

They have here propertied me: keep me in darkness, send ministers to me—asses—and do all they can to face me out of my wits.

Feste

Advise you what you say: the minister is here.

95 [*Speaking as Sir Topas*] Malvolio, Malvolio, thy wits the heavens restore: endeavour thyself to sleep, and leave thy vain bibble babble.

Malvolio

Sir Topas!

Feste

[*As Sir Topas*] Maintain no words with him, good

100 fellow! [*As himself*] Who, I, sir? Not I, sir! God buy you, good Sir Topas! [*As Sir Topas*] Marry, amen! [*As himself*] I will, sir, I will.

Malvolio

Fool, fool, fool, I say!

Feste

Alas, sir, be patient. What say you, sir? I am shent

105 for speaking to you.

Malvolio

Good fool, help me to some light and some paper: I tell thee I am as well in my wits as any man in Illyria.

109   *Well-a-day that*: alas, if only.

111   *convey ... down*: carry the letter that I shall write.
111–13   *It shall ... did*: you will get more for this than you have ever got for carrying letters.

115   *counterfeit*: pretend.

119   *requite it*: reward you for it.
      in the highest degree: to the utmost.
121–29   Feste's song has not been identified, but such verses are often found in the Morality Plays of the 15th and 16th centuries where a stock character was the *Vice*. He accompanied the Devil, sometimes as his mate or even his son; and he was often armed with a wooden sword (*dagger of lath*), with which he would sometimes cut the Devil's nails and drive him from the stage.

121   *anon*: at once.
123   *trice*: moment.
      old: i.e. in the old plays.
124   *sustain*: satisfy.
128   *Pare*: cut.
129   *Adieu*: goodbye.
      goodman: good master.

Feste
Well-a-day that you were, sir!

Malvolio
110 By this hand, I am! Good fool, some ink, paper, and light, and convey what I will set down to my lady. It shall advantage thee more than ever the bearing of letter did.

Feste
I will help you to't. But tell me true, are you not
115 mad indeed or do you but counterfeit?

Malvolio
Believe me, I am not. I tell thee true.

Feste
Nay, I'll ne'er believe a madman till I see his brains. I will fetch you light, and paper, and ink.

Malvolio
Fool, I'll requite it in the highest degree. I prithee,
120 be gone.

Feste
      I am gone, sir, and anon, sir,
            I'll be with you again,
      In a trice, like to the old Vice,
            Your need to sustain;
125   Who, with dagger of lath, in his rage
                        and his wrath,
            Cries, 'Ah, ha!' to the devil:
      Like a mad lad, 'Pare thy nails, dad.
            Adieu, goodman devil!'   [*Exit*

Act 4   Scene 3
Sebastian is puzzled because he cannot find Antonio; he is further surprised when Olivia enters with a priest, demanding that he should go with her to the nearby chapel and formally agree to marry her.

6   *there he was*: he had been there.
    credit: information.
7   *range*: wander around.
9   *my soul ... sense*: my mind

Scene 3 Olivia's *garden*

Enter Sebastian

Sebastian
This is the air, that is the glorious sun,
This pearl she gave me, I do feel't, and see't,
And though 'tis wonder that enwraps me thus,
Yet 'tis not madness. Where's Antonio then?
5 I could not find him at the Elephant.
Yet there he was, and there I found this credit,

agrees with the evidence of my senses.

10   'There may have been some mistake, but I am not mad.'

11   *flood of fortune*: excessively good luck.

12   *instance*: precedent.
      discourse: explanation.

14   *wrangle*: argue.

15   *trust*: belief.

17   *sway her house*: govern the household.
      followers: servants.

18   'Undertake (*Take*) business (*affairs*), and see that things get done (*give back their dispatch* to the *affairs*).'

19   'In such a calm, sensible, and poised manner.'

21   *deceivable*: deceptive.

24   *chantry*: chapel—these were often attached to great houses.
      by: nearby.

25   *underneath . . . roof*: inside that hallowed building.

26   *Plight . . . faith*: give me complete assurance of your intentions. Olivia is demanding that Sebastian should 'plight his troth' to her; when this was done in the presence of a witness, it formed a contract as binding as marriage.

27   *jealous*: possessive.
      doubtful: insecure, suspicious.

28   *He*: i.e. the 'holy man', their witness.

29   *Whiles*: until.
      come to note: be made public.

30   *What time*: at which time.
      our celebration keep: celebrate our marriage ceremony.

31   *According to my birth*: in a manner suitable to my social position.
      What do you say: do you agree.

33   *having sworn truth*: when I have promised to be true (i.e. in plighting his troth).
      ever: always.

34   *father*: the proper form of address to a priest.

35   *fairly note*: look favourably upon.

That he did range the town to seek me out.
His counsel now might do me golden service:
For though my soul disputes well with my sense
10 That this may be some error, but no madness,
Yet doth this accident and flood of fortune
So far exceed all instance, all discourse,
That I am ready to distrust mine eyes,
And wrangle with my reason that persuades me
15 To any other trust but that I am mad,
Or else the lady's mad; yet if 'twere so,
She could not sway her house, command her followers,
Take and give back affairs and their dispatch,
With such a smooth, discreet, and stable bearing
20 As I perceive she does. There's something in't
That is deceivable. But here the lady comes.

Enter Olivia *and* Priest

Olivia
Blame not this haste of mine. If you mean well,
Now go with me and with this holy man
Into the chantry by; there before him,
25 And underneath that consecrated roof,
Plight me the full assurance of your faith,
That my most jealous and too doubtful soul
May live at peace. He shall conceal it
Whiles you are willing it shall come to note,
30 What time we will our celebration keep
According to my birth. What do you say?
Sebastian
I'll follow this good man, and go with you,
And having sworn truth, ever will be true.
Olivia
Then lead the way, good father, and heavens so shine,
35 That they may fairly note this act of mine!

[*Exeunt*

Act 5

Act 5   Scene 1

Feste, carrying Malvolio's letter and going in search of Olivia, jests with Orsino and Viola/Cesario. The officers bring Antonio before Orsino, and Antonio tells how he has risked his life to search for the young man who now rejects him. The complications increase when Olivia arrives and claims her newly-betrothed husband, 'Cesario'. The jealous Orsino at first threatens to harm the youth who seems to have betrayed him, but then Olivia's priest confirms the marriage-contract. Sir Andrew and Sir Toby appear, both having been wounded in their fight with Sebastian—who now comes on to the scene. Slowly he and Viola identify each other. At last Feste delivers Malvolio's letter to Olivia, and the steward is released from his prison.

1   *his*: i.e. Malvolio's letter to Olivia, written from his prison.

5–6   An Elizabethan courtier, John Manningham, records in his *Diary* an anecdote concerning Queen Elizabeth and a relative of hers, Dr Bullein, who was very fond of his dog. The Queen requested that Dr Bullein should grant her one desire, and she promised to give him whatever it was that *he* wanted in return. Elizabeth demanded the dog; Dr Bullein gave it to her, and asked Her Majesty to fulfil her part of the bargain. 'I will,' agreed Queen Elizabeth. 'Then I pray you,' said Dr Bullein, 'give me my dog again'.

7   *Belong you*: are you from the household of.

8   *trappings*: ornaments.

15   *they*: i.e. friends.
         make an ass: i.e. by praising him.

Scene 1 *The street*

Enter Feste *and* Fabian

Fabian
Now as thou lov'st me, let me see his letter.

Feste
Good Master Fabian, grant me another request.

Fabian
Anything.

Feste
Do not desire to see this letter.

Fabian
5 This is to give a dog, and in recompense desire my dog again.

Enter Orsino, Viola, Curio, *and* Lords

Orsino
Belong you to the Lady Olivia, friends?

Feste
Ay, sir, we are some of her trappings.

Orsino
I know thee well. How dost thou, my good fellow?

Feste
10 Truly, sir, the better for my foes, and the worse for my friends.

Orsino
Just the contrary: the better for thy friends.

Feste
No, sir: the worse.

Orsino
How can that be?

Feste
15 Marry, sir, they praise me, and make an ass of me. Now my foes tell me plainly I am an ass: so that by my foes, sir, I profit in the knowledge of myself, and by my friends I am abused. So that, conclu-

17   *profit ... myself*: gain self-knowledge.

18   *abused*: deceived.

18–9   *conclusions to be as kisses*: assume that the conclusions drawn from any argument are like kisses taken from a girl. Feste may now be referring to the poem *Astrophil and Stella*, by Sir Philip Sidney; Stella refuses her lover's request for a kiss and 'Lest once should not be heard, twice said "No no"'. Astrophil argues that two negatives make an affirmative, so that 'No no' means 'Yes'. Feste's reference to the *four negatives* and *two affirmatives* has no more logical sense.

26   *But that ... double-dealing*: if it did not involve duplicity (deceit).
        I would: I wish.

27   *it:* i.e. the gold coin.

28   *ill counsel*: bad advice (in recommending duplicity).

29–30   *grace ... flesh and blood*: grace comes from God and is the divine means whereby man can overcome the moral weaknesses of his human flesh and blood. 'To put (something) in one's pocket' was an idiomatic phrase meaning 'deliberately to overlook or forget (it)'. Feste urges Orsino (who, being a duke is properly addressed as 'your grace') to listen to his 'ill counsel' and put not only his 'grace' but also his hand (*your flesh and blood*) into his pocket—where he keeps his money.

33   *Primo, secundo, tertio*: first, second, third (Latin); Feste probably alludes to a children's game (*play*).

33–4   *the old saying*: i.e. 'third time lucky'—used to encourage gamblers who have failed twice to make a third attempt.

34   *triplex*: triple time in music.

35   *tripping measure*: skipping rhythm.
        Saint Bennet: the church of St Benedict (there was in fact such a church—St Bennet Hithe—just opposite Shakespeare's Globe Theatre).

36   *put you in mind*: jog your memory.

sions to be as kisses, if your four negatives make your two affirmatives, why then the worse for my friends, and the better for my foes.

Orsino

Why, this is excellent.

Feste

By my troth, sir, no—though it please you to be one of my friends.

Orsino

25 Thou shalt not be the worse for me: there's gold.

Feste

But that it would be double-dealing, sir, I would you could make it another.

Orsino

O, you give me ill counsel.

Feste

Put your grace in your pocket, sir, for this once, and

30 let your flesh and blood obey it.

Orsino

Well, I will be so much a sinner to be a double-dealer; there's another.

Feste

Primo, secundo, tertio, is a good play, and the old saying is 'The third pays for all'; the triplex, sir, is a

35 good tripping measure; or the bells of Saint Bennet, sir, may put you in mind—one, two, three.

Orsino

You can fool no more money out of me at this throw. If you will let your lady know I am here to speak with her, and bring her along with you, it

40 may awake my bounty further.

Feste

Marry, sir, lullaby to your bounty till I come again. I go, sir, but I would not have you to think that my desire of having is the sin of covetousness. But as you say, sir, let your bounty take a nap, I will awake

45 it anon.   [*Exit*

Enter Antonio *and* Officers

Viola

Here comes the man, sir, that did rescue me.

Orsino

That face of his I do remember well;

37   *fool*: trick.
38   *throw*: throw of the dice.
40   *bounty*: generosity.
41   *lullaby to your bounty*: may your generosity sleep well.
42-3   *my desire of having*: Feste offers no reason why this should be any different from *the sin of covetousness*.
45   *anon*: very soon.

49   *Vulcan*: the Roman god of blacksmiths.
50   *baubling vessel*: miserable little boat.
51   *For shallow draught*: very light-weight; the *draught* is the depth of water needed to float a vessel.
      bulk unprizable: of no value, not worth taking as a prize.
52   *such . . . make*: he got into such a damaging (*scathful*) engagement (*grapple*).
53   *bottom*: vessel.
54   'That even those who envied him, and the voices of those who had lost in the fight.'
55   *Cried . . . on him*: praised and honoured him.
57   *took*: captured.
      fraught: cargo, freight.
      Candy: Candia (now called Crete).
60   *desperate . . . state*: reckless of his own honour or the position he was in.
61   *brabble*: brawl.
      apprehend: arrest.
62   *drew on my side*: drew his sword to fight on my behalf.
63   *in conclusion*: afterwards.
      put . . . upon me: spoke very oddly to me.
64   *distraction:* madness.
65   *Notable*: notorious.
      salt-water thief: robber on the seas.
66   *to their mercies*: into the hands of those men.
67   *in terms . . . dear*: in such bloody and deadly circumstances.

Yet when I saw it last, it was besmear'd
As black as Vulcan, in the smoke of war.
50 A baubling vessel was he captain of,
For shallow draught and bulk unprizable,
With which such scathful grapple did he make
With the most noble bottom of our fleet,
That every envy and the tongue of loss
55 Cried fame and honour on him. What's the matter?
First Officer
Orsino, this is that Antonio
That took the *Phoenix* and her fraught from Candy,
And this is he that did the *Tiger* board,
When your young nephew Titus lost his leg.
60 Here in the streets, desperate of shame and state,
In private brabble did we apprehend him.
Viola
He did me kindness, sir, drew on my side,
But in conclusion put strange speech upon me,
I know not what 'twas, but distraction.
Orsino
65 Notable pirate, thou salt-water thief,
What foolish boldness brought thee to their mercies
Whom thou in terms so bloody and so dear
Hast made thine enemies?

69   *Be pleas'd*: please let me.
        shake off: reject.
71   *base and ground enough*: with
very good reason.
72   *A witchcraft ... hither*: I came
here because I was bewitched (i.e. he
was enchanted by his love for
Sebastian; cf. Olivia's words to Viola
(3.1.111) referring to 'the last
enchantment you did here').
73   *ingrateful*: ungrateful.
74   *rude*: rough.
75   *redeem*: rescue.
        A wrack ... was: he was
hopelessly shipwrecked.
77   *retention* reservation.
78   *All ... dedication*: I completely
devoted myself to him.
79   *pure for his love*: entirely for
love of him.
80   *adverse*: hostile.
81   *Drew*: i.e. drew my sword.
        beset: attacked.
82   *Where being apprehended*: and
when I was arrested at this time.
83   *partake ... danger*: share the
danger with me.
84   *face ... acquaintance*: deny that
he had any knowledge of me.
85   *grew ... thing*: became like one
who had not been near me for twenty
years.
86   *While ... wink*: in the twinkling
of an eye, in an instant.
        denied: refused to give me.
87   *recommended ... use*: persuaded
him to take for his own use.
90   *three months*: Shakespeare is not
particularly consistent in his references
to time in this play.
91   *No int'rim*: without a break.
        vacancy: space.
92   *keep company*: stay together.
93   *heaven ... earth*: Orsino
compares Olivia to a goddess.
95   *tended upon*: attended on,
served.
96   *anon*: presently.
97   *but ... have*: except for that
which he may not have (i.e. her love).
98   'In which Olivia can be of
assistance.'

Antonio   Orsino, noble sir,
Be pleas'd that I shake off these names you give me:
70 Antonio never yet was thief, or pirate,
Though I confess, on base and ground enough,
Orsino's enemy. A witchcraft drew me hither:
That most ingrateful boy there by your side,
From the rude sea's enrag'd and foamy mouth
75 Did I redeem. A wrack past hope he was.
His life I gave him, and did thereto add
My love, without retention or restraint,
All his in dedication. For his sake
Did I expose myself—pure for his love—
80 Into the danger of this adverse town;
Drew to defend him, when he was beset;
Where being apprehended, his false cunning
(Not meaning to partake with me in danger)
Taught him to face me out of his acquaintance,
85 And grew a twenty years' removed thing
While one would wink; denied me mine own purse,
Which I had recommended to his use
Not half an hour before.
Viola   How can this be?
Orsino
When came he to this town?
Antonio
90 Today, my lord and for three months before
No int'rim, not a minute's vacancy,
Both day and night did we keep company.

Enter Olivia *and Attendants*

Orsino
Here comes the Countess: now heaven walks on
    earth!
But for thee, fellow—fellow, thy words are
    madness.
95 Three months this youth hath tended upon me;
But more of that anon. Take him aside.
Olivia
What would my Lord—but that he may not have—
Wherein Olivia may seem serviceable?
Cesario, you do not keep promise with me.
Viola
100 Madam?

99   *keep promise with*: keep your promise to.

104   *aught to the old tune*: the same old stuff.

105   *fat and fulsome*: boring and sickening.

106   *howling*: i.e. the howling of a dog.

108   *uncivil*: rude, discourteous.

109   *ingrate*: ungrateful.
        unauspicious: unrewarding.

111   *e'er devotion tender'd*: ever offered in devotion.

112   *Even what*: whatever.
        become: be suitable for.

113–14 Orsino refers to the story of Thyamis, an Egyptian bandit who kidnapped the lady Chariclea whom he loved; he tried to kill her rather than let her be taken away from him. The story was told by Heliodorus in his *Ethiopica*, which was widely read (in translation) in the sixteenth century.

116   *sometimes savours nobly*: has some touches of nobility in it.
        hear me this: just let me say this.

117   *non-regardance*: contempt.

118   *that*: since.
        partly know: have some idea of.

119   *screws*: wrenches.
        true: rightful.

120   *marble-breasted*: hard-hearted.

121   *minion*: darling.

122   *tender*: hold, care for.

123–24 Orsino threatens to remove his page from Olivia's sight, since in her eyes (which are *cruel* to Orsino), Cesario is like a king (*sits crowned*), to the vexation of Orsino (*in his master's spite*).

125   *ripe in mischief*: ready to do injury.

127   *a raven's heart ... dove*: a cruel black heart within a gentle body. The contrast between ravens and doves is common in Elizabethan literature.

128   *jocund*: cheerful.
        apt: ready.

129   *To do you rest*: to bring you peace.

Orsino
Gracious Olivia—
    Olivia
What do you say, Cesario? [*To* Orsino] Good my lord—
    Viola
My lord would speak; my duty hushes me.
    Olivia
If it be aught to the old tune, my lord,
105 It is as fat and fulsome to mine ear
As howling after music.
    Orsino
Still so cruel?
    Olivia   · Still so constant, lord.
    Orsino
What, to perverseness? You uncivil lady,
To whose ingrate and unauspicious altars
110 My soul the faithfull'st off'rings hath breath'd out
That e'er devotion tender'd—What shall I do?
    Olivia
Even what it please my lord that shall become him.
    Orsino
Why should I not, had I the heart to do it,
115 Like to th' Egyptian thief at point of death,
Kill what I love?—a savage jealousy
That sometimes savours nobly! But hear me this:
Since you to non-regardance cast my faith,
And that I partly know the instrument
That screws me from my true place in your favour,
120 Live you the marble-breasted tyrant still.
But this your minion, whom I know you love,
And whom, by heaven, I swear I tender dearly,
Him will I tear out of that cruel eye
Where he sits crowned in his master's spite.
125 Come, boy, with me; my thoughts are ripe in mischief:
I'll sacrifice the lamb that I do love,
To spite a raven's heart within a dove.
    Viola
And I most jocund, apt, and willingly,
To do you rest, a thousand deaths would die.
    Olivia
130 Where goes Cesario?

132   *by all mores*: by all such comparisons.
       than ... wife: than I shall ever love a wife.
133–34   'If I speak falsely (*feign*), may the gods above (who are the *witnesses* of the vow) punish me with death for being disloyal to (*tainting of*) the one I love.'
135   *Ay me detested*: Oh I am accursed.
       beguil'd: deceived.
136   *do you wrong*: injure you.

141   *sirrah*: a contemptuous form of address.
142   *the baseness ... fear*: your miserable cowardice.
143   *strangle thy propriety*: suppress your real identity (i.e. as Olivia's husband).
144   *take ... up*: assume your proper place in life.
145   *Be that*: be what.
146   *as that thou fear'st*: as great as the man (i.e. Orsino) that you are afraid of.
147   *charge*: order.
       by thy reverence: in all your holiness.
148   *unfold*: reveal.
       lately: recently.
149   *in darkness*: hidden.
       occasion: the circumstances.
151   *newly pass'd*: recently taken place.
153   *joinder*: joining.
154   *Attested*: demonstrated.
       the holy close of lips: a holy kiss.
155   *interchangement*: exchange.
157   *Seal'd in my function*: made official by me as a priest.
       testimony: formal statement.
158–59   *toward ... hours*: I am only two hours older.

Viola   After him I love
More than I love these eyes, more than my life,
More, by all mores, than e'er I shall love wife.
If I do feign, you witnesses above
Punish my life, for tainting of my love.
Olivia
135   Ay me detested! How am I beguil'd!
Viola
Who does beguile you? Who does do you wrong?
Olivia
Hast thou forgot thyself? Is it so long?
Call forth the holy father.   [*Exit an Attendant*
Orsino   Come, away!
Olivia
Whither, my lord? Cesario, husband, stay!
Orsino
140   Husband?
Olivia   Ay, husband. Can he that deny?
Orsino
Her husband, sirrah?
Viola   No, my lord, not I.
Olivia
Alas, it is the baseness of thy fear
That makes thee strangle thy propriety.
Fear not, Cesario, take thy fortunes up,
145   Be that thou know'st thou art, and then thou art
As great as that thou fear'st.

Enter Priest

                              O welcome, father!
Father, I charge thee by thy reverence
Here to unfold—though lately we intended
To keep in darkness what occasion now
150   Reveals before 'tis ripe—what thou dost know
Hath newly pass'd between this youth and me.
Priest
A contract of eternal bond of love,
Confirm'd by mutual joinder of your hands,
Attested by the holy close of lips,
155   Strengthen'd by interchangement of your rings,
And all the ceremony of this compact
Seal'd in my function, by my testimony;
Since when, my watch hath told me, toward my

160

160   *dissembling*: lying.
       cub: young fox (the fox is
proverbially cunning).

161   'By the time you are old.'
       time: age.
       sow'd: scattered.
       a grizzle: some grey hairs.
       case: head (*or* beard; *or* a fox's
skin).

162–63 'Or perhaps you will get so
cunning that you will trip yourself up
and ruin yourself.'

163   *trip*: a leg movement in
wrestling which is intended to throw
the opponent to the ground.

164–65 'Make sure that our paths never
cross.'

167   *Hold little faith*: keep at least a
little faith (i.e. confidence).

168   *presently*: immediately.

> grave
> I have travell'd but two hours.
>
> **Orsino**
>
> 160 O thou dissembling cub! What wilt thou be
> When time hath sow'd a grizzle on thy case?
> Or will not else thy craft so quickly grow
> That thine own trip shall be thine overthrow?
> Farewell, and take her; but direct thy feet
> 165 Where thou and I henceforth may never meet.
>
> **Viola**
>
> My lord, I do protest—
>
> **Olivia**   O do not swear!
> Hold little faith, though thou hast too much fear.
>
> *Enter* Sir Andrew
>
> **Sir Andrew**
>
> For the love of God, a surgeon! Send one presently
> to Sir Toby.
>
> **Olivia**
>
> 170 What's the matter?

171   'Has broke ... across: he has hit me over the head.
172   coxcomb: head.
173   'I would give any amount of money to be at home' (as at 2.3.20, no specific amount is intended: forty = a lot of).
175–76 took him for: thought he was.
176   incardinate: Sir Andrew mistakes the word 'incarnate' = 'in human form'.
178   'Od's lifelings: by God's life (the diminutive plural 'lifelings' reduces the strength of the oath).
178–79 for nothing: for no reason.
179   that that I did: whatever it was that I did.
        set on to do't: persuaded to do it.
183   bespake you fair: answered you courteously.
185   set nothing by: think nothing of.
186   halting: limping.
187   in drink: drunk.
187–88 tickled you othergates: dealt with you differently.
189   How is't with you: what's wrong with you.
190   That's all one: that doesn't matter.
        'has: he has.
190–91 there's th'end on't: that's all there is to it.
191   Sot: fool.
        Dick Surgeon: i.e. Dick the surgeon.
192   an hour agone: for the past hour.
193   set: closed (in a drunken stupor).
        eight i'th' morning: eight o'clock this morning.
194   passy measures pavin: Sir Toby knows a lot about dance (see 1.3.120–25), and here he seems to be reviling the drunken surgeon with the name of a dance, the passe-measure pavane. The pavane is a stately dance with sequences of eight bars (Feste's reference to 'eight' may have prompted this to Sir Toby).
198–99 we'll be dressed: we will have our wounds dressed.

Sir Andrew
'Has broke my head across, and has given Sir Toby a bloody coxcomb too. For the love of God, your help! I had rather than forty pound I were at home.
Olivia
Who has done this, Sir Andrew?
Sir Andrew
175 The Count's gentleman, one Cesario. We took him for a coward, but he's the very devil incardinate.
Orsino
My gentleman, Cesario?
Sir Andrew
'Od's lifelings, here he is! You broke my head for nothing; and that that I did, I was set on to do't by
180 Sir Toby.
Viola
Why do you speak to me? I never hurt you.
You drew your sword upon me without cause,
But I bespake you fair, and hurt you not.

Enter Sir Toby *and* Feste

Sir Andrew
If a bloody coxcomb be a hurt, you have hurt me: I
185 think you set nothing by a bloody coxcomb. Here comes Sir Toby halting; you shall hear more. But if he had not been in drink, he would have tickled you othergates than he did.
Orsino
How now, gentleman? How is't with you?
Sir Toby
190 That's all one; 'has hurt me, and there's th' end on't. Sot, didst see Dick Surgeon, sot?
Feste
O, he's drunk, Sir Toby, an hour agone; his eyes were set at eight i' th' morning.
Sir Toby
Then he's a rogue, and a passy-measures pavin. I
195 hate a drunken rogue.
Olivia
Away with him! Who hath made this havoc with them?
Sir Andrew
I'll help you, Sir Toby, because we'll be dressed

together.

Sir Toby

200 Will you help? An ass-head, and a coxcomb, and a
knave, a thin-faced knave, a gull!

Olivia

Get him to bed, and let his hurt be looked to.
[*Exeunt* Feste, Fabian, Sir Toby, *and* Sir Andrew

Enter Sebastian

Sebastian

I am sorry, madam, I have hurt your kinsman:
But had it been the brother of my blood,

205 I must have done no less with wit and safety.
You throw a strange regard upon me, and by that
I do perceive it hath offended you:
Pardon me, sweet one, even for the vows
We made each other but so late ago.

Orsino

210 One face, one voice, one habit, and two persons!
A natural perspective, that is, and is not!

200 *coxcomb*: idiot.
201 *gull*: dupe.

202 *looked to*: taken care of.

204 *brother of my blood*: kinsman.
205 *with wit and safety*: with any
sensible concern for my own safety.
206 *You ... me*: you are looking at
me very oddly.
208 *even for*: especially because of.
209 *but so late ago*: only very
recently.
210 *habit*: costume.
211 *perspective*: distorting-glass—an
artificial device to produce optical
illusions—but this one is *natural*.
that ... not: it seems like an
illusion, and yet it is not.

213   *rack'd*: dragged out (as though he were tortured on the rack).

215   *Fear'st thou*: do you doubt.

216   *made ... yourself*: divided yourself in two.
217   *cleft*: split.

221–22   'And I do not have the divine power of being everywhere at once.'
223   *blind*: i.e. pitiless, because they could not see what they were doing.
224   *Of charity*: be kind and tell me.
       kin: relation.
225   *What countryman*: what is your nationality.
228   *So ... suited*: he was dressed like this when he went.

229–30   'If devils can appear in mortal shapes and clothing.' The next line suggests that Viola is using *spirits* here in the common Elizabethan sense (= devils), although Sebastian immediately rejects that meaning when he uses *spirit* to mean 'immortal soul'.
231   *dimension*: bodily frame.
       grossly: solidly.
232   *from the womb*: from my birth.
       participate: share in (with the rest of mankind).
233   *as ... even*: as it appears from everything else (i.e. except the clothing).

238–39   'And died on my thirteenth birthday.'
240   *record*: memory.
       lively: vivid.
241   *his mortal act*: his life.

Sebastian
Antonio! O my dear Antonio,
How have the hours rack'd and tortur'd me,
Since I have lost thee!
          Antonio
215 Sebastian are you?
          Sebastian   Fear'st thou that, Antonio?
          Antonio
How have you made division of yourself?
An apple cleft in two is not more twin
Than these two creatures. Which is Sebastian?
          Olivia
Most wonderful!
          Sebastian
220 Do I stand there? I never had a brother;
Nor can there be that deity in my nature
Of here and everywhere. I had a sister,
Whom the blind waves and surges have devour'd.
Of charity, what kin are you to me?
225 What countryman? What name? What parentage?
          Viola
Of Messaline. Sebastian was my father;
Such a Sebastian was my brother too:
So went he suited to his watery tomb.
If spirits can assume both form and suit,
230 You come to fright us.
          Sebastian   A spirit I am indeed,
But am in that dimension grossly clad
Which from the womb I did participate.
Were you a woman, as the rest goes even,
I should my tears let fall upon your cheek
235 And say, 'Thrice welcome, drowned Viola.'
          Viola
My father had a mole upon his brow.
          Sebastian
And so had mine.
          Viola
And died that day when Viola from her birth
Had number'd thirteen years.
          Sebastian
240 O, that record is lively in my soul!
He finished indeed his mortal act
That day that made my sister thirteen years.

243   *lets*: hinders.
244   'Except this masculine costume which I have no right to wear.'
246   *cohere and jump*: fit exactly and agree.
249   *Where*: i.e. in whose keeping.
      maiden weeds: female clothes.
      whose: i.e. the captain's.
251   'Everything that has happened to me since then'.
252   *between*: concerned with.
253   *So comes it*: that is how it happened.
      been mistook: made a mistake.
254   'Nature corrected that mistake in her own way.' Shakespeare takes his metaphor from the game of bowls, where the *bias* is both the lead weight inside the bowl to prevent its going straight, and the curved path which it then follows.
255   *contracted to a maid*: married to a girl.
256–57 Sebastian swears by his life that Olivia has not been cheated of being married to a 'maid' (*therein ... deceiv'd*) by the fact that he himself is alive.
257   *both ... man*: i.e. to a man who is a virgin (*maid*).
258   *amaz'd*: worried.
      right ... blood: he is of truly noble birth.
259   *as yet ... true*: since this is not a deceiving 'perspective' (cf. line 211).
260   *most happy wreck*: very lucky shipwreck.
262   *like to me*: as much as you love me.
263   *over-swear*: swear again (with repeated emphasis).
265   *As doth ... the fire*: as truly as the sun (*that orbed continent*) maintains its fire.
266   *severs*: separates.
267   *weeds*: dress.
269   *action*: legal charge.
270   *in durance*: under arrest.
      at Malvolio's suit: on the accusation of Malvolio.
271   *follower*: servant.

Viola
If nothing lets to make us happy both,
But this my masculine usurp'd attire,
245 Do not embrace me, till each circumstance
Of place, time, fortune, do cohere and jump
That I am Viola; which to confirm
I'll bring you to a captain in this town,
Where lie my maiden weeds; by whose gentle help
250 I was preserv'd to serve this noble Count.
All the occurrence of my fortune since
Hath been between this lady and this lord.
   Sebastian
[*To* Olivia] So comes it, lady, you have been mistook.
But nature to her bias drew in that.
255 You would have been contracted to a maid;
Nor are you therein, by my life, deceiv'd:
You are betroth'd both to a maid and man.
   Orsino
Be not amaz'd; right noble is his blood.
If this be so, as yet the glass seems true,
260 I shall have share in this most happy wreck.
[*To* Viola] Boy, thou hast said to me a thousand times
Thou never should'st love woman like to me.
   Viola
And all those sayings will I over-swear,
And all those swearings keep as true in soul
265 As doth that orbed continent the fire
That severs day from night.
   Orsino   Give me thy hand,
And let me see thee in thy woman's weeds.
   Viola
The captain that did bring me first on shore
Hath my maid's garments. He upon some action
270 Is now in durance at Malvolio's suit,
A gentleman and follower of my lady's.
   Olivia
He shall enlarge him: fetch Malvolio hither.
And yet alas, now I remember me,
They say, poor gentleman, he's much distract.

   Enter Feste *with a letter, and* Fabian

272   *enlarge him*: set him free.
273   *now I remember me*: I have just remembered.
278   *much distract*: very disturbed in his mind.
275–76 'A madness (*frenzy*) of my own which took everything out of my mind obviously drove his madness from my memory.'
277   *How does he*: how is he.
278–79 *he holds ... end*: he is fighting off the devil (*Beelzebub*). The expression was proverbial; and the metaphor is from the sport of quarterstaff fighting—keeping one's opponent at a safe distance.
278   *stave's end*: the end of the staff.
279   *in his case*: in his condition.
        'Has: he has.
280–81 *today morning*: this morning.
281–83 *epistles ... delivered*: in these lines Feste makes play with the specifically religious senses of some of the words: *epistles* are the apostolic letters in the New Testament of the Bible, and the *gospels* are the four apostolic accounts of the life of Christ. There was argument in the sixteenth century concerning the exact moment in the church service when the gospels should be read aloud (*delivered*) to the congregation.
281   *epistles*: letters.
282   *gospels*: words of truth.
        skills not: does not matter.
285   *Look then*: prepare.
        edified: enlightened.
285–86 *delivers the madman*: speaks the words of the madman.

275 A most extracting frenzy of mine own
    From my remembrance clearly banish'd his.
    How does he, sirrah?

    Feste
    Truly, Madam, he holds Beelzebub at the stave's end as well as a man in his case may do. 'Has here
280 writ a letter to you—I should have given't you to-day morning, but as a madman's epistles are no gospels, so it skills not much when they are delivered.

    Olivia
    Open't, and read it.

    Feste
285 Look then to be well edified, when the fool delivers the madman. [*Reads like a madman*] *By the Lord, madam—*

    Olivia
    How now, art thou mad?

    Feste
    No, madam, I do but read madness: an' your
290 ladyship will have it as it ought to be, you must allow *vox*.

289   *I ... madness*: I am only reading madness.
        an: if.
291   *allow vox*: let me use the proper voice (Latin *vox* = voice).

292   *i' thy right wits*: in a proper state of mind.

293   *his right wits*: i.e. Malvolio's state of mind.

294   *thus*: i.e. in Malvolio's absurd phrasing.
   perpend: pay attention (Feste is about to use Malvolio's manner).

295   *give ear*: listen.

299   *rule*: command.

301   *induced*: persuaded.

302   *semblance*: appearance.

304–05   *I leave . . . of*: I am forgetting the respect which I owe to you.

305   *speak . . . injury*: address you so boldly because of the wrong that has been done to me.

308   *savours . . . distraction*: does not sound much like madness.

309   *See him deliver'd*: see to it that he is released.

310–11   'My lord, now that we have been able to think things over (*these things further thought on*), be pleased to accept me (*think me as well*) for a sister as much as you would have liked me as a wife.'

312   *one day*: the same day.
   crown: celebrate.
   th'alliance on't: the relationship formed by the double wedding.

313   *my proper cost*: my own expense.

314   *apt*: ready.

315   *quits you*: releases you from service.

316   *mettle of your sex*: feminine nature.

317   *soft and tender breeding*: gentle upbringing (as a noble lady).

Olivia

Prithee, read i' thy right wits.

Feste

So I do, madonna. But to read his right wits is to read thus: therefore, perpend, my princess, and
295 give ear.

Olivia

[*To Fabian*] Read it you, sirrah.

Fabian

[*Reads*]

> By the Lord, madam, you wrong me, and the world shall know it. Though you have put me into darkness, and given your drunken cousin rule over
300 me, yet have I the benefit of my senses as well as your ladyship. I have your own letter that induced me to the semblance I put on; with the which I doubt not but to do myself much right, or you much shame. Think of me as you please. I leave my duty a little
305 unthought of, and speak out of my injury.
> > The madly-used Malvolio

Olivia

Did he write this?

Feste

Ay, madam.

Orsino

This savours not much of distraction.

Olivia

See him deliver'd, Fabian, bring him hither.

[*Exit* Fabian

310 My lord, so please you, these things further thought on,
To think me as well a sister, as a wife;
One day shall crown th' alliance on't, so please you,
Here at my house, and at my proper cost.

Orsino

Madam, I am most apt t'embrace your offer.
315 [*To Viola*] Your master quits you; and for your service done him,
So much against the mettle of your sex,
So far beneath your soft and tender breeding,
And since you call'd me master for so long,
Here is my hand; you shall from this time be
320 Your master's mistress.

320   *A sister*: Olivia will now have (in Viola) a sister of her own.

323   *Notorious*: outrageous.

324   *peruse*: study.
325   *hand*: handwriting.
326   *Write from it*: write in a different way.
       in hand: in handwriting.
       phrase: style.
327   *your invention*: composed by you.
328   *grant*: admit.
329   *in the modesty of honour*: decently and honourably.
330   *clear lights*: unmistakeable signs.
331   *Bade*: ordered.
333   *lighter*: inferior.
334   *acting this*: when I did this.
335   *suffer'd*: allowed.
337   *geck and gull*: fool and dupe.
338   *invention*: trickery.
339   *this ... writing*: I did not write this.
340   *character*: handwriting.
341   *out of question*: without a doubt.
       hand: handwriting
342   *bethink me*: remember.
343   *cam'st*: i.e. cam'st thou.
344   *forms*: ways.
344–45 *presuppos'd Upon*: suggested beforehand to you.
346   'This trick (*practice*) has been played on (*pass'd upon*) you in a very malicious way (*most shrewdly*).'
347   *grounds*: reasons.
       authors: those responsible.

350   *to come*: that will happen in the future.
351   *Taint*: spoil.
       the condition: i.e. the happiness.

Olivia   A sister! You are she.

Enter Fabian *with* Malvolio

Orsino
Is this the madman?
Olivia   Ay, my lord, this same.
How now, Malvolio?
Malvolio   Madam, you have done me wrong,
Notorious wrong.
Olivia   Have I, Malvolio? No!
Malvolio
Lady, you have. Pray you, peruse that letter.
325 You must not now deny it is your hand:
Write from it, if you can, in hand or phrase,
Or say 'tis not your seal, not your invention.
You can say none of this. Well, grant it then,
And tell me, in the modesty of honour,
330 Why you have given me such clear lights of favour,
Bade me come smiling and cross-garter'd to you,
To put on yellow stockings, and to frown
Upon Sir Toby, and the lighter people?
And acting this in an obedient hope,
335 Why have you suffer'd me to be imprison'd,
Kept in a dark house, visited by the priest,
And made the most notorious geck and gull
That e'er invention play'd on? Tell me, why?
Olivia
Alas, Malvolio, this is not my writing,
340 Though I confess much like the character:
But, out of question, 'tis Maria's hand.
And now I do bethink me, it was she
First told me thou wast mad; then cam'st in smiling,
And in such forms which here were presuppos'd
345 Upon thee in the letter. Prithee, be content;
This practice hath most shrewdly pass'd upon thee.
But when we know the grounds and authors of it,
Thou shalt be both the plaintiff and the judge
Of thine own cause.
Fabian   Good madam, hear me speak,
350 And let no quarrel, nor no brawl to come,
Taint the condition of this present hour,
Which I have wonder'd at. In hope it shall not,

354   *Set this device against*: played
this trick on.
355   *Upon*: because of.
stubborn ... parts: obstinate and
discourteous behaviour.
356   *We had ... him*: which had
turned us against him.
writ: wrote.
357   *importance*: importunity.
358   *In recompense whereof*: as a
reward for which.
359   *How*: the way.
sportful: playful.
it: i.e. Maria's letter to
Malvolio.
360   *pluck on*: provoke.
361   *If that*: if.
justly: fairly.
362   *pass'd*: been suffered.
363   *poor fool*: Olivia speaks
compassionately to Malvolio.
baffled thee: treated you
disgracefully.
366   *interlude*: entertainment.
one Sir Topas: a certain Sir
Topas.
367   *that's all one*: that isn't
important.
368–70   *Madam ... gagged*: Feste recalls
Malvolio's words early in the play
(1.5.81–6).
370   *whirligig*: spinning-top.
371   *his*: its.
373   *notoriously abus'd*: shamefully
misused.
375   *of*: about.
376   *convents*: is convenient.
377   *solemn combination*: religiously
formal union (i.e. their marriage).
378   *sweet sister*: Orsino accepts
Olivia's invitation (lines 310–11).
381   *habits*: clothes (i.e. her female
dress).
382   *fancy's*: love's.
383   *When ... and*: when I was only.

385   *toy*: trifle (his silly tricks were
not taken seriously).

Most freely I confess, myself and Toby
Set this device against Malvolio here,
355   Upon some stubborn and uncourteous parts
We had conceiv'd against him. Maria writ
The letter, at Sir Toby's great importance,
In recompense whereof he hath married her.
How with a sportful malice it was follow'd
360   May rather pluck on laughter than revenge,
If that the injuries be justly weigh'd
That have on both sides pass'd.
Olivia
Alas, poor fool, how have they baffled thee!
Feste
Why, 'Some are born great, some achieve great-
365   ness, and some have greatness thrown upon them.'
I was one, sir, in this interlude, one Sir Topas, sir—
but that's all one. 'By the Lord, fool, I am not mad.'
But do you remember: 'Madam, why laugh you at
such a barren rascal; an' you smile not, he's
370   gagged'? And thus the whirligig of time brings in
his revenges.
Malvolio
I'll be reveng'd on the whole pack of you!   [*Exit*
Olivia
He hath been most notoriously abus'd.
Orsino
Pursue him, and entreat him to a peace.
375   He hath not told us of the captain yet.
                                   [*Exit* Fabian
When that is known, and golden time convents,
A solemn combination shall be made
Of our dear souls. Meantime, sweet sister,
We will not part from hence. Cesario, come—
380   For so you shall be while you are a man.
But when in other habits you are seen.
Orsino's mistress, and his fancy's queen.
                          [*Exeunt all except* Feste
Feste
When that I was and a little tiny boy,
   With hey, ho, the wind and the rain,
385   *A foolish thing was but a toy,*
   For the rain it raineth every day.

387   *came to man's estate*: grew up to
be a man.

But when I came to man's estate,
  With hey, ho, the wind and the rain,
'Gainst knaves and thieves men shut their gate,
  For the rain it raineth every day.

390

391   *to wive*: to take a wife.

But when I came, alas, to wive,
  With hey, ho, the wind and the rain,
By swaggering could I never thrive,
  For the rain it raineth every day.

393   *swaggering*: boasting.
      thrive: succeed.

395   *came ... beds*: got much older.   395

But when I came unto my beds,
  With hey, ho, the wind and the rain,
With toss-pots still 'had drunken heads,
  For the rain it raineth every day.

397   'Like other drunkards (*toss-
pots*) I always had a hang-over.'

415

A great while ago the world begun,
  With hey, ho, the wind and the rain,
But that's all one, our play is done,
  And we'll strive to please you every day.

400

401   *that's all one*: that doesn't
matter now.
402   *We'll strive ... day*: the signal
for the audience to applaud now that
the 'play is done'.

[*Exit*

Appendix

O mistress mine

When that I was

O mistress mine

1. O mis-tress mine, where are you roam-ing?
2. What is love? 'Tis not here-af-ter,

O stay and hear, your true love's co-ming, O stay and
Pre-sent mirth hath pre-sent laugh-ter: Pre-sent

hear, your true love's co-ming, That can sing both high and
mirth hath pre-sent laugh-ter: What's to come is still un-

low. Trip no fur-ther, pret-ty sweet-ing: Jour-neys
-sure. In de-lay there lies no plen-ty, Then come

end in lo-vers meet-ing, Ev-'ry wise man's son doth know.
kiss me, sweet and twen-ty: Youth's a stuff will not en-dure.

When that I was

When that I was and a lit-tle ti-ny boy, With a

hey-ho, the wind and the rain, A fool-ish thing was

but a toy, For the rain it rain-eth

ev-'ry day, With a hey-ho, the

wind and the rain, For the rain it rain-eth ev-'ry day.

Classwork and Examinations

The works of Shakespeare are studied all over the world, and this classroom edition is being used in many different countries. Teaching methods vary from school to school and there are many different ways of examining a student's work. Some teachers and examiners expect detailed knowledge of Shakespeare's text; others ask for imaginative involvement with his characters and their situations; and there are some teachers who want their students to share in the theatrical experience of directing and performing a play. Most people use a variety of methods. This section of the book offers a few suggestions for approaches to *Twelfth Night* which could be used in schools and colleges to help with students' understanding and *enjoyment* of the play.

A Discussion
B Character Study
C Activities
D Context Questions
E Comprehension Questions
F Essays
G Projects

A   Discussion

Talking about the play — about the issues it raises and the characters who are involved — is one of the most rewarding and pleasurable aspects of the study of Shakespeare. It makes sense to discuss each scene as it is read, sharing impressions — and perhaps correcting misapprehensions. It can be useful to compare aspects of this play with other fictions — plays, novels, films — or with modern life.

Suggestions

A1   What kind of entertainment would you choose to celebrate some special occasion?

A2 'What should *I* do in Illyria?' (*1*, 2, 3). Viola is stranded all alone in a strange country – what would *you* do in such a situation?

A3 We hear a lot about Olivia before the character herself comes on to the stage. What kind of person do you expect to see?

A4 Orsino counsels Viola on the choice of a marriage-partner: 'Let still the woman take An elder to herself' (2, 4, 29–30). What is your opinion of this advice?

A5 What kind of costume would you use for *Twelfth Night*? Could the play be performed in modern dress?

A6 The name given to this play in the First Folio is *Twelfth Night, or, What you Will*. Can you suggest any better titles?

B   Character Study

Shakespeare is famous for his creation of characters who seem like real people. We can judge their actions and we can try to understand their thoughts and feelings — just as we criticize and try to understand the people we know. As the play progresses, we learn to like or dislike, love or hate, them — just as though they lived in *our* world.

Characters can be studied *from the outside*, by observing what they do, and listening sensitively to what they say. This is the scholar's method: the scholar — or any reader — has access to the whole play, and can see the function of every character within the whole scheme of that play.

Another approach works *from the inside*, taking a single character and looking at the action and the other characters from his/her point of view. This is the way an actor prepares for performance, creating a character who can have only a partial view of what is going on; and it asks for a student's inventive imagination. The two methods — both useful in different ways — are really complementary to each other.

Suggestions

a) from 'outside' the character

B1 The text does not give much information about the *ages* of the characters, and the director can have a fairly free hand. Suggest the ages of

a) Viola, Sebastian, Olivia, and Orsino
b) Maria, Sir Toby, and Sir Andrew
c) Malvolio.

B2 Describe the character and function of Feste.

B3 Make detailed character-studies of
a) Orsino
b) Olivia
c) Malvolio.

B4 Do you agree that Sir Toby and Sir Andrew are both rather pathetic characters?

B5 'The most decent people in this play are the two sea-captains, who both show "a fair behaviour" (*1*, 2, 47) that is quite unlike the conduct of the other characters.' Do you agree?

B6 Show how the character of Olivia changes as the play progresses.

B7 'One face, one voice, one habit, and two persons' (*5*, 1, 210). Contrast the characters of Viola and Sebastian.

b) from 'inside' a character

B8 The sea-captain tells Viola that his tongue will not 'blab' about her doings in Illyria. But he writes to his wife at home, describing the twins who were passengers on his recent voyage, and the storm that wrecked his ship.

B9 Maria writes a letter to her friend, describing life at Olivia's house.

B10 In her diary, Olivia describes Duke Orsino and the messengers whom he sends to her — including the latest, 'Cesario'.

B11 Sir Andrew decides to 'stay a month longer' (*1*, 3, 105) — but he must write home, to explain what he is doing, and to get some more money.

B12 Malvolio prepares a written report on the various misdoings of Sir Toby and his companions.

B13 The Clown seems to be all things to all men (and women) — but what is he when he is alone? Write Feste's memoirs, *People in my Life*, or, *Thoughts in Isolation*.

B14 In the character of Antonio, describe (in your diary) your thoughts and feelings when you saw the re-union of Sebastian and Viola.

B15 'I'll be reveng'd on the whole pack of you' (5, 1, 372). In the character of Malvolio, plot your revenge.

C Activities

These can involve two or more students, preferably working *away from* the desk or study-table and using gesture and position ('body-language') as well as speech. They can help students to develop a sense of drama and the dramatic aspects of Shakespeare's play — which was written to be *performed*, not studied in a classroom.

Suggestions

C1 Curio and Valentine, having a drink in the buttery, discuss Orsino and his passion for Olivia.

C2 Maria says (*1*, 3, 14) that she has heard Olivia talk about Sir Toby and his friend. Devise a scene where Maria is present as lady-in-waiting when Olivia tells a friend about her troublesome kinsman.

C3 Using your own words, act out the comic scenes (e.g. *Act 1*, Scene 3, and *Act 3*, Scene 4) between Sir Toby, Sir Andrew, and Maria. Give your scenes a wholly modern setting and idiom.

C4 In *Act 2*, Scene 4 Orsino and Viola compare men's love with the love of women. Express their ideas — and develop the argument — in your own words.

C5 Improvise a scene where Viola describes her 'fight' with Sir Andrew to amuse her brother, Orsino, and Olivia.

C6 Cover aspects of the story — 'Twins Rescued from Shipwreck', 'She Wooed for the Man she Would Win', 'Which did she Wed?' — for the local newspapers.

C7 The double wedding is to have full coverage from all the media — newspapers, radio, and television. If possible, arrange signing for the deaf — and translations (or sub-titles) for foreign-language speakers. Get interviews with *everybody* — including those who want to appear on television but have nothing to tell you.

C8   Act the play — or at least parts of it (e.g. 'the letter scene' — *Act 2*, Scene 5 — and the twins' reunion in *Act 5*).

D   Context Questions

In written examinations, these questions present you with short passages from the play, and ask you to explain them. They are intended to test your knowledge of the play and your understanding of its words. Usually you have to make a choice of passages: there may be five on the paper, and you are asked to choose three. Be very sure that you know exactly how many passages you must choose. Study the ones offered to you, and select those you feel most certain of. Make your answers accurate and concise — don't waste time writing more than the examiner is asking for.

D1   I will not be so hard-hearted; I will give out divers schedules of my beauty. It shall be inventoried, and every particle and utensil labelled to my will: as — item, two lips, indifferent red; item, two grey eyes, with lids to them; item, one neck, one chin, and so forth.

  (i)   Who says this? To whom? At what point in the play?
  (ii) What had the person spoken to just said to provoke these lines in reply? Comment on the kind of words used here and explain the effect the speaker wants them to have.

D2   I hate ingratitude more in a man
Than lying, vainness, babbling drunkenness,
Or any taint of vice whose strong corruption
Inhabits our frail blood.

  (i)   Who has been accused of ingratitude, and by whom?
  (ii) Why was a mistake made?
  (iii) Explain the meaning of 'babbling drunkenness'.

D3   Be not afraid, good youth. I will not have you.
And yet, when wit and youth is come to harvest,
Your wife is like to reap a proper man.

  (i)   Who is speaking, and who is the 'good youth'?
  (ii) What is meant by 'reap a proper man'?
  (iii) Are the speaker's words likely to come true?

D4 Why, man, he's the very devil; I have not seen such a virago. I
had a pass with him, rapier, scabbard and all; and he gives me
the stuck-in with such a mortal motion that it is inevitable.

  (i) Who is the 'very devil' referred to? Who is speaking of
  him, and to whom does he speak?
  (ii) What is meant by 'had a pass'?
  (iii) Whom does the listener attack, and with what result?

D5   Diana's lip
Is not more smooth and rubious. Thy small pipe
Is as the woman's organ, shrill and sound,
And all is semblative a woman's part.

  (i) Who is the speaker and whom does he address?
  (ii) Who was 'Diana'?
  (iii) What is referred to as a 'small pipe'?

E   Comprehension Questions

These also present passages from the play and ask questions about
them; again you often have a choice of passages. But the extracts are
much longer than those presented as context questions. A detailed
knowledge of the language of the play is asked for here, and you
must be able to express unusual or archaic phrases in your own
words; you may also be asked to comment critically on the
effectiveness of Shakespeare's language.

E1 This fellow is wise enough to play the fool,
And to do that well craves a kind of wit.
He must observe their mood on whom he jests,
The quality of persons, and the time,
And, like the haggard, check at every feather   5
That comes before his eye. This is a practice
As full of labour as a wise man's art.
For folly that he wisely shows is fit;
But wise men, folly-fall'n, quite taint their wit.

  (i) Who is the speaker, and who is the 'fellow' referred to?
  (ii) Explain the meaning of 'quality of persons', 'haggard',
  and 'folly-fall'n'.
  (iii) In your own words, express the meaning of 'like the

haggard, check at every feather That comes before his eye'.

(iv) What do these lines show about the speaker's attitude to people who 'play the fool'?

E2 'What is your parentage?'
'Above my fortunes, yet my state is well;
I am a gentleman.' I'll be sworn thou art:
Thy tongue, thy face, thy limbs, actions and spirit
Do give thee five-fold blazon. Not too fast: soft! soft!   5
Unless the master were the man — How now?
Even so quickly may one catch the plague?
Methinks I feel this youth's perfections
With an inevitable and subtle stealth
To creep in at mine eyes.   10

(i) Give the exact context of this speech, naming 'the master' and 'the man'.
(ii) What is a 'blazon'?
(iii) What does this speech show us about the speaker?
(iv) How do the lines express the speaker's emotions?

E3 Wit, an't be thy will, put me into good fooling. Those wits that think they have thee do very oft prove fools; and I that am sure I lack thee may pass for a wise man. For what says Quinapulus — 'better a witty fool than a foolish wit'.

(i) Who is the speaker? What is his occupation?
(ii) Which characters in the play 'prove fools'?
(iii) What aspect of the play does this speech draw attention to?

E4 Disguise, I see thou art a wickedness
Wherein the pregnant enemy does much.
How easy is it for the proper false
In women's waxen hearts to set their forms.
Alas, our frailty is the cause, not we,   5
For such as we are made of, such we be,
How will this fadge?

(i) Who is speaking and what has just happened?
(ii) How does it 'fadge'?
(iii) What is meant by 'the pregnant enemy' and 'the proper false'?
(iv) Comment on Shakespeare's imagery in these lines.

F   Essays

These will usually give you a specific topic to discuss, or perhaps a question that must be answered, in writing, *with a reasoned argument*. They *never* want you to tell the story of the play — so don't! Your examiner — or teacher — has read the play and does not need to be reminded of it. Relevant quotations will always help you to make your points more strongly.

F1 'The greatest lover in the play is not Orsino, nor even Viola, but Antonio.' Do you agree?

F2 Mistaken identity in *Twelfth Night*.

F3 'Although it is a happy comedy, there is great deal of hurt in this play.' Do you share this opinion.

F4   Methinks I feel this youth's perfections
With an invisible and subtle stealth
To creep in at mine eyes.

Describe the various feelings and the aspects of her character that Olivia shows in her meetings with Viola.

F5 'Dost thou think because thou art virtuous there shall be no more cakes and ale?' Contrast the different attitudes of Sir Toby and Malvolio.

F6 'For such as I am, all true lovers are.' Is Orsino the best model of a 'true lover'?

F7 'I am as mad as he If sad and merry madness equal be.' Give examples from the play of 'sad and merry madness'.

F8 Should we pity Olivia or laugh at her?

G   Projects

In some schools, students are asked to do more 'free-ranging' work, which takes them outside the text — but which should always be relevant to the play. Such Projects may demand skills other than reading and writing; design and artwork, for instance, may be involved. Sometimes a 'portfolio' of work is assembled over a considerable period of time; and this can be presented to the examiner as part of the student's work for assessment.

  The availability of resources will, obviously, do much to

determine the nature of the Projects; but this is something that only the local teachers will understand. However, there is always help to be found in libraries, museums, and art galleries.

Suggested Subjects

G1 Twelfth Night.

G2 Famous Actresses in *Twelfth Night*.

G3 The Elizabethan Clown.

G4 The Elizabethan Household.

G5 Elizabethan Popular Songs.

Background

England c. 1600

When Shakespeare was writing *Twelfth Night*, most people believed that the sun went round the earth. They were taught that this was a divinely ordered scheme of things, and that — in England — God had instituted a Church and ordained a Monarchy for the right government of the land and the populace.

'The past is a foreign country; they do things differently there.'

L.P. Hartley

Government

For most of Shakespeare's life, the reigning monarch of England was Queen Elizabeth I. With her counsellors and ministers, she governed the country (population about five million) from London, although fewer than half a million people inhabited the capital city. In the rest of the country, law and order were maintained by the land-owners and enforced by their deputies. The average man had no vote, and his wife had no rights at all.

Religion

At this time, England was a Christian country. All children were baptized, soon after they were born, into the Church of England; they were taught the essentials of the Christian faith, and instructed in their duty to God and to humankind. Marriages were performed, and funerals conducted, only by the licensed clergy and in accordance with the Church's rites and ceremonies. Attendance at divine service was compulsory; absences (without good — medical — reason) could be punished by fines. By such means, the authorities were able to keep some check on the populace — recording births, marriages, and deaths; being alert to any religious nonconformity, which could be politically dangerous; and ensuring a minimum of orthodox instruction through the official 'Homilies' which were regularly preached from the pulpits of all parish churches throughout the realm. Following Henry VIII's break away from the Church of Rome, all people in England were able to hear the church services *in their own language*. The Book of Common Prayer was used in every church, and an English translation of the Bible was read aloud in public. The Christian religion had never been so well taught before!

Education

School education reinforced the Church's teaching. From the age of four, boys might attend the 'petty school' (French *'petite école'*) to learn the rudiments of reading and writing along with a few prayers; some schools also included work with numbers. At the age of seven, the boy was ready for the grammar school (if his father was willing and able to pay the fees).

Here, a thorough grounding in Latin grammar was followed by translation work and the study of Roman authors, paying attention as much to style as to matter. The arts of fine writing were thus inculcated from early youth. A very few students proceeded to university; these were either clever scholarship boys, or else the sons of noblemen. Girls stayed at home, and acquired domestic and social skills — cooking, sewing, perhaps even music. The lucky ones might learn to read and write.

Language

At the start of the sixteenth century the English had a very poor opinion of their own language: there was little serious writing in English, and hardly any literature. Latin was the language of international scholarship, and Englishmen admired the eloquence of the Romans. They made many translations, and in this way they extended the resources of their own language, increasing its vocabulary and stretching its grammatical structures. French, Italian, and Spanish works were also translated, and — for the first time — there were English versions of the Bible. By the end of the century, English was a language to be proud of: it was rich in synonyms, capable of infinite variety and subtlety, and ready for all kinds of word-play — especially the *puns*, for which Shakespeare's English is renowned.

Drama

The great art-form of the Elizabethan age was its drama. The Elizabethans inherited a tradition of play-acting from the Middle Ages, and they reinforced this by reading and translating the Roman playwrights. At the beginning of the sixteenth century, plays were performed by groups of actors, all-male companies (boys acted the female roles) who travelled from town to town, setting up their stages in open places (such as inn-yards) or, with the permission of the owner, in the hall of some noble house. The touring companies continued, in the provinces, into the seventeenth century; but in London, in 1576, a new building was erected for the performance of plays. This was the Theatre, the first purpose-built playhouse in England. Other playhouses followed, (including Shakespeare's own theatre, the Globe) and the English drama reached new heights of eloquence.

There were those who disapproved, of course. The theatres, which brought large crowds together, could encourage the spread of disease — and dangerous ideas. During the summer, when the plague was at its worst, the playhouses were closed. A constant censorship was imposed, more or less severe at different times. The Puritan faction tried to close down the theatres, but — partly because there was royal favour for the drama, and partly because the buildings were outside the city limits — they did not succeed until 1642.

Theatre

From contemporary comments and sketches — most particularly a drawing by a Dutch visitor, Johannes de Witt — it is possible to form some idea of the typical Elizabethan playhouse for which most of Shakespeare's plays were written. Hexagonal in shape, it had three roofed galleries encircling an open courtyard. The plain, high stage projected into the yard, where it was surrounded by the audience of standing 'groundlings'. At the back were two doors for the actors' entrances and exits; and above these doors was a balcony — useful for a musicians' gallery or for the acting of scenes *above*. Over the stage was a thatched roof, supported on two pillars, forming a canopy — which seems to have been painted with the sun, moon, and stars for the 'heavens'. Underneath was space (concealed by curtaining) which could be used by characters ascending and descending through a trap-door in the stage. Costumes and properties were kept backstage, in the 'tiring house'. The actors dressed lavishly, often wearing the secondhand clothes bestowed by rich patrons. Stage properties were important for defining a location, but the dramatist's own words were needed to explain the time of day, since all performances took place in the early afternoon.

Selected Further Reading

Barber, C.L., *Shakespeare's Festive Comedy*, (Princeton, NJ, 1959).
Hotson, Leslie, *The First Night of 'Twelfth Night'*, (London, 1954).
Leggatt, Alexander, *Shakespeare's Comedy of Love*, (London, 1974).
Muir, Kenneth, *The Sources of Shakespeare's Plays*, (London, 1977).
Palmer, D.J., 'Art and Nature in *Twelfth Night*', *Critical Quarterly*, 9 (1967), pp. 210–12.
Potter, Lois, *Twelfth Night* (Text and Performance Series; London, 1983).
Salingar, L.G., *Shakespeare and the Traditions of Popular Comedy*, (Cambridge, 1974).

Background Reading

Blake, N.F., *Shakespeare's Language: an Introduction*, (Methuen, 1983).
Muir, K., and Schoenbaum, S., *A New Companion to Shakespeare Studies*, (Cambridge, 1971).
Schoenbaum, S., *William Shakespeare: A Documentary Life*, (Oxford, 1975).
Thomson, Peter, *Shakespeare's Theatre*, (Routledge and Kegan Paul, 1983).